www.mascotbooks.com

The Brooklyn Suppers: Creating Community with Seasonal Fare

For more information, please contact:
Mascot Books
620 Herndon Parkway, Suite 320
Herndon, VA 20170
info@mascotbooks.com

Library of Congress Control Number: 2021914414

CPSIA Code: PRQ0921A
ISBN-13: 978-1-64543-447-4

Printed in Malaysia

The Brooklyn Suppers

Creating Community with Seasonal Fare

Heather Antonelli

For Kate.

"Twenty years from now, you will be more disappointed by the things you didn't do than by the ones you did. So throw off the bowlines. Sail away from the safe harbor. Catch the trade winds in your sails. Explore. Dream. Discover."
Mark Twain

Introduction

When you move to Brooklyn, New York, with only your one-year-old Weimaraner and a few suitcases, what do you do to make friends fast? You feed them!

Once settled into my three-story walk-up, I spent a few months nesting and decorating. While walking Sula several times a day, I started checking out my insanely cool new neighborhood, which is filled with sidewalk cafes, trendy new restaurants, boutique clothing stores, wine bars, and a few seedy bars too. My kind of town.

Finding and making friends was hard, but pop-up supper clubs had just become a thing and were trending fast. What better way to meet people outside of a bar setting? Being the lonely girl sitting at the bar is never a good thing.

I started attending supper clubs in my surrounding neighborhoods. I made friends. I had unique experiences you couldn't find anywhere else in the world.

I love to entertain and have done so since college. I also love to cook, especially for others, so I started my very own supper club. I originally called it Two Bridges Supper Club, as my apartment was near both the Brooklyn and Manhattan Bridges, and a lot of my guests were reaching my apartment via one of these bridges, if they weren't already living in Brooklyn. I later changed the name to The Brooklyn Suppers, purely to emphasize what I was doing in Brooklyn. Many of my guests were coming from the city and had never actually been to Brooklyn. My suppers changed a lot of their opinions about Brooklyn, and I was proud to be a part of that.

The Brooklyn Suppers is organized by actual calendar order. A few were hosted at my mother's glamping farm in Georgia, as locals from her community saw what I was doing on social media and wanted me to host dinners there as well. How could I say no?

The best way to enjoy the recipes is really up to you! You can create your own suppers with friends and family, following my themes and menus, or you can use the book as a tool for making dinner at home with your family, picking and choosing recipes best suited to your style. No matter how you choose to use the book, I hope you make as many wonderful memories as I have.

Grazie,
Heather

Tips for Hosting

1. Invitations

Any proper gathering deserves an invitation. Whether it's via email, post, or hand-delivered, some form of invitation outside of a verbal one is necessary.

2. Plan Ahead

Plan the menu before doing anything else. When planning, ask yourself if the dishes fit the season, the type of guests you have invited, and your actual cooking abilities.

3. Don't Be a Hero

Do not try to make dishes that you have never made, seen, or tasted. It's fun to experiment when cooking, but it is not quite as much fun when you realize you are in over your head and guests are en route.

4. Make a List

Write down the menu. Then write down every ingredient you are going to need to buy that isn't already in your pantry or refrigerator.

5. Quality over Quantity

Choose high-quality, fresh ingredients over sale items that may be past their freshness dates. This is not the time to go on the cheap.

6. Prep Ahead

The more prep work you can do before anyone arrives (without sacrificing freshness) the better.

7. Fresh Flowers

Always have fresh seasonal flowers around the house and on the dining table. It can be as simple as a few tulips in spring or a few sprigs of holly in winter.

8. Set the Table

Always have the table set before guests arrive. If you are taking the time to host, take the time to have the house clean and the table set.

9. Employ a Greeter

Ask a friend or hire staff to be a greeter for your event. You are way too busy to answer the door, take coats (if necessary), show guests to the living or dining room, or take drink orders. A greeter can also be tasked with making sure the guest bathroom is well maintained. (See #12, The Guest Bathroom.) When the evening comes to a close, a greeter can also present coats and see guests out the door without disturbing you or your other guests.

10. Employ a Server

The greeter can also be your hired server. Once everyone has arrived and the meal begins, your former greeter can then become the server for the event. You do not have time to cook, plate, and serve while actually being the host or hostess of your event.

11. No Person Hungry

Once your guests have arrived and your greeter has given everyone the beverage of their choice, understand that hunger has set in. You do not want overly hungry guests. Have a small hors d'oeuvre ready on a tray that is easy for the greeter to offer guests as they mingle prior to sitting down to the table.

12. The Guest Bathroom

Always be sure your guest bathroom is clean and your greeter/server is looking after it. Provide two or three clean hand towels on the counter or a nearby hook. Have a clean, pleasant-smelling pump hand soap by the sink. No one wants to share a bar of soap, yes? Provide a room spray that is not too flowery and not too masculine. A scent like fresh laundry is the best. Lastly, have a small vase with fresh white flowers on the counter. During your event, have your greeter check on the bathroom at least twice to tidy up, if needed.

13. Pets

While we love our furry family members, not everyone else does. Keep your pets in a bedroom or other room so they won't interact with your guests.

14. No Hostages

While you might want the night to go on forever, your guests may not. Be respectful of time and keep a tight schedule from arrival to cocktails, dinner, dessert, and an optional nightcap. Think two and a half to three hours, then set them free.

15. A Keepsake

After a wonderful event, you want to send your guests off with a small token of thanks for attending. It can be as simple as a baked good elegantly wrapped or a few nice chocolates in a small box with a pretty ribbon. If you are really ambitious, attach a little note saying thank you or including a nice quote.

The Suppers

Winter White

Scallopops

**Masala-Spiced Black Cod, Coconut Milk, Basil,
Oyster Mushroom, Quinoa**

Grilled White Asparagus, Dijon Vinaigrette

Vanilla Bean Panna Cotta

Serves 4

The Meal

The idea for my Winter White Supper was to create the feeling that we brought a snowy day inside. It was cozy and casual. The food reflected the weather outside, with clean white and cream tones, but it was warming to eat. The light fare left guests feeling restored and healthy. It was the new beginning of a New Year.

The New Year still had plenty of white snow on the ground and in the gardens. My brownstone had a nice backyard that was completely covered in snow and was truly a winter wonderland with the tree branches covered in ice drooping over onto blankets of white snow. Sula, after being patient through the supper, was let outside. Guests, now gathered in the kitchen, all got a great laugh at her eating the snow and bounding across the yard back to the warmth with her big floppy ears leading the way!

The Theme

I love watching the snow fall gently past the windows and settling onto the ground. I love being beside a big fire while watching the snow fall. I love cooking on snowy days, all bundled up inside with a delicious meal. It's all made better if friends show up and we share a Winter White Supper.

After supper, everyone bundled up and headed out into the snow for a walk, breathing in the cold winter air and feeling the snowflakes on our cheeks.

There is no place more magical to see it snow than Brooklyn. The brownstones were covered in what looked like white icing on gingerbread, and you could hear the laughter and cheer coming from inside each bar and restaurant. The streets were otherwise silent, and the tiny little snow globe we were in seemed like a miracle.

The Setup

The table décor was white, off-white, and cream. The textures were soft cottons and knobby knits with white plates and napkins. White flowers like paperwhites and delicate white tulips adorned the table in small cream-colored ceramic vases. I served prosecco in tall glass flutes as guests arrived. There were cream-colored taper candles in delicate glass candleholders down the table, and the main overhead lights were dimmed to create a relaxing environment. Keeping it clean and simple but fresh and new was the feeling I was going for.

Winter White

The Brooklyn Suppers

Scallopops

- 8 fresh sea scallops, rinsed and patted dry
- ½ cup olive oil, plus 1 Tbsp, divided
- 1 ½ cup panko breadcrumbs
- 1 tsp each ground black pepper, salt, chili powder, and ground ginger
- 1 tsp white pepper
- 1 tsp fresh thyme
- ½ cup crème fraîche
- 4 wooden skewers

Step one: Pour a glass of chilled prosecco. That's for you.

Lightly coat each scallop with 1 tablespoon of olive oil.

Mix panko, pepper, salt, chili, and ginger in a bowl.

Coat both sides of each scallop with panko mix.

In a shallow sauté pan, warm ½ cup olive oil until lightly sizzling.

Add scallops and cook on both sides for 6 minutes each. Scallops should be cooked through and crusted on the outside. Transfer from pan to serving plate or platter.

Insert a skewer from the side of each scallop, creating a lollipop (or scallopop). Layer two scallops on each skewer.

In the same pan as scallops were cooked, add white pepper, thyme, and crème fraîche. Stir until blended and just shy of bubbling.

Remove from heat and cool slightly.

Pour sauce over scallopops in a drizzle, not a bath.

Serve.

The Brooklyn Suppers

Masala-Spiced Black Cod, Coconut Milk, Basil, Oyster Mushroom, Quinoa

- 2 lb black cod (can substitute white cod if necessary)

- 2 Tbsp olive oil, divided

- ½ cup garam masala spice mix*

- 2 tsp fresh garlic, chopped fine

- 3 cipollini onions, chopped fine

- 1 (16-oz) can coconut milk

- 2 cups fresh basil, torn into pieces (keep 4 tsp aside for garnish)

- 2 cups oyster mushrooms, stemmed

- 2 cups bonnet mushrooms, stemmed

- 1 lemon

- 4 cups cooked quinoa (substitute couscous, jasmine rice, or angel hair pasta, if desired)

Garam masala is a blend of spices and chilis from northern India. It can be bought in stores or made from scratch.

Rinse cod, pat dry, and coat with 1 tablespoon olive oil.

Coat fish with garam masala. To add extra heat to the dish, apply a heavier coating of the spice mix.

Heat 1 tablespoon of olive oil in a deep sauté pan.

Add garlic and onions to the pan. Stir until soft, about 5 minutes.

Add fish and cook on each side for 5 minutes.

Add coconut milk, basil, and mushrooms to the pan.

Simmer, covered, over medium-low heat for 20 minutes, turning fish after 10 minutes. Fish should be tender and crumbling when ready.

Transfer fish to individual plates or serving platter.

Pour pan sauce over fish, making sure each plate gets an equal amount of basil and mushrooms.

Squeeze lemon over top, and garnish with fresh black pepper. Serve with quinoa.

Grilled White Asparagus, Dijon Vinaigrette

- 1 tsp Dijon mustard

- 1 Tbsp olive oil

- 1 Tbsp white balsamic vinegar

- 1 tsp each fresh ground black pepper and salt

- 12 stalks white asparagus

Combine mustard, olive oil, vinegar, pepper, and salt in a mixing bowl and whisk until uniform in color and texture.

With a vegetable peeler, remove the single outer layer of asparagus, starting two-thirds of the way down the stalk.

Coat asparagus with vinaigrette.

Grill asparagus over medium-high heat until tender, turning often.

In a saucepan over medium heat, heat remaining vinaigrette and stir until heated through.

Serve asparagus on a platter with vinaigrette drizzled over the top.

Vanilla Bean Panna Cotta

- 1 cup whole milk

- 1 Tbsp powdered gelatin, unflavored

- 3 cups whipping cream

- ⅓ cup honey

- ⅓ cup white sugar

- 1 fresh vanilla bean, scraped from pod

- Pinch salt

- 2 cups fresh blackberries

In a small bowl, combine milk and gelatin. Let stand for 5 minutes.

Pour the mixture into a heavy saucepan, and stir over medium heat until gelatin has dissolved.

Add cream, honey, sugar, vanilla bean, and salt to the saucepan.

Stir another 5 minutes, then remove from heat.

Pour the mixture into 4–6 individual ramekins, let cool slightly.

Refrigerate ramekins until the mixture is fully set, about 6 hours.

Remove and garnish with the fresh blackberries before serving.

Amuse Bouche

Smoked Black Cod Carpaccio
with Fried Capers,
Grapefruit, Celery Fronds;
Drizzled with White Truffle Olive Oil

Roasted Fennel & Spring Onion,
Rucola & Buffalo Mozz Insalata with Pesto

Balsamic Baked Quail
on a bed of Cannellini
with Caramelized Vidalias,
Spinach, Sun Dried Tomatoes & Fried Shallots

Cider Braised Pork
with Smashed New Potatoes
& a Spicy Tomatoe Chutney

Plum, Pear Ricotta Bruschetta
with Chocolate Fig Marmalade

Assorted Cheeses, Membrillo,
Torta de Aceite, Port

Primavera

Bresaola, Basil, and Cherry Goat Cheese Bites

Amuse-Bouche (Chilled Cucumber Cilantro Soup)

Balsamic Quail, Cannellini, Caramelized Vidalia, Sun Dried Tomatoes, Fried Shallots

Cider Braised Pork Butt, Smashed New Potatoes, Spicy Tomato Chutney

Plum Pear Ricotta Bruschetta, Chocolate Fig Marmalade

Smoked Cod Carpaccio, Fried Capers, Grapefruit, Celery Fronds, Truffle Oil

Assorted Cheeses, Membrillo, Torta De Aceite, Port

Roasted Fennel, Spring Onion, Rucola, Buffalo Mozzarella, Pesto

Serves 4

The Meal

Primavera Supper was all about celebrating spring's early gifts from the gardens and decadent dishes to awaken our taste buds and our appetites for the year ahead. This supper was a total of eight dishes, each evoking some feeling of indulgence with at least one ingredient. Tender flavors like grapefruit, fennel, and smoked cod felt light and healthy, while the quail and chocolate fig marmalade let us feel a bit naughty. Most guests brought champagne or white wine, which were the perfect accompaniments to the indulgent dishes. Keeping the portions of each course quite small allowed the guests to really enjoy the flavors of each course without filling up.

The guests were all in such great cheer as the supper came to a close. No one was getting up to leave. The wine was running low, but the conversations were only getting livelier. For the first time at one of the suppers, a guest suggested that everyone go to a local bar for a nightcap and to keep the conversations going. They asked me for a few suggestions and off everyone went to keep the night alive. As I began to tackle cleanup, I stopped for a moment and just relished in the fact that my goal of bringing strangers together to share a meal had ended with new friendships.

The Theme

After being cooped up inside all winter, spring brought a new energy to Brooklyn. The parks were filled with joggers, strollers, children, dogs, picnickers, bikers, and families and friends enjoying the turn of the season. Spring bulbs were blooming, and the snow gave way to fresh green grass. Primavera Supper celebrates all things spring!

The Setup

Primavera's table was delicately decorated with white wedding chairs, light green napkins in a trellis print, and tiny bouquets of pink roses in clear glass vases across the length of the table. A packet of spring seeds at each place setting as a takeaway gift gave color to the table and elicited smiles from the guests. The table was meant to feel as light as the mood of the guests who all were so ready to enjoy the warm weather and be out socializing again after the long winter.

Bresaola, Basil, and Cherry Goat Cheese Bites

- 4 slices dried bresaola, halved

- ½ cup goat cheese

- 4 fresh basil leaves, finely chopped

- ½ cup dried cherries

- 1 pinch each of salt and pepper

- 8 chive strings

Lay out bresaola slices on a cutting board.

Combine goat cheese with basil and cherries with a hand mixer. Blend well.

Season the mixture with salt and pepper.

Place 1 teaspoon goat cheese mixture in center of each bresaola square.

Pull up corners of each square and tie with chive string to create a small bundle.

Place bundles on a serving tray, and garnish with basil bits.

Serve.

Amuse-Bouche
(Chilled Cucumber Cilantro Soup)

- 12 Castelvetrano olives, separated

- 1 small cucumber, peeled and roughly chopped

- 1 Tbsp cilantro, roughly chopped (can substitute Italian parsley)

- 1 pinch each of salt and pepper

Roughly chop four olives and add to blender. Set aside remaining olives for garnish.

Add cucumber, cilantro, salt, and pepper to blender.

Blend ingredients until smooth.

Chill at least 1 hour. While soup chills, skewer remaining 8 olives with 4 toothpicks (2 olives per toothpick).

Pour soup into small glasses (juice or Moroccan tea size), and garnish with skewered olives.

Serve.

Balsamic Quail, Cannellini, Caramelized Vidalia, Sun Dried Tomatoes, Fried Shallots

- 2 cloves garlic, roughly chopped

- 1 ½ cups fresh rosemary, chopped and divided

- 4 quail, rinsed and patted dry

- Pinch each of ground salt and pepper

- 2 cups balsamic vinegar, divided

- 2 cups canned cannellini beans

- ¼ cup fresh rosemary, roughly chopped

- ½ cup olive oil

Place ¼ of chopped garlic and ¼ of chopped rosemary into the cavity of each quail.

Season exterior of birds with salt and pepper.

Brush birds with balsamic vinegar until fully coated.

Heat oven to 350°F and roast birds for 30 minutes, brushing every 10 minutes with more balsamic vinegar as it dries out.

Remove birds and let rest 10 minutes.

Pour the cannellini beans and the canned liquid into a saucepan and cook through at a low temperature. Add ¼ cup fresh rosemary to the beans with salt and pepper, to taste.

In a small frying pan, add Vidalia onions and ¼ cup olive oil and cook until onions begin to soften. Add 2 Tbsp balsamic vinegar and cook until vinegar is absorbed and onions are soft and sticky.

The Brooklyn Suppers

- 4 Vidalia onions, cut vertically into ¼-inch slices

- 4 cups fresh spinach leaves

- 2 cups cherry tomatoes, whole

- 4 shallots, cut vertically into ¼-inch slices

Remove onions from pan and add spinach. Add ¼ cup of olive oil and cook until spinach is wilted.

Toss tomatoes in olive oil and roast them in a roasting pan (frying pan can be used as substitution) in the oven at 350°F until soft, approximately 15 minutes.

In a clean frying pan, add a splash of olive oil and shallots.

Cook over high heat until shallots are crunchy and fried.

Place ¼ of the wilted spinach on each plate.

Spoon equal amounts of the cannellini beans and onions over spinach.

Place quail on top of bean mixture.

Place equal amounts of the tomatoes on one side of each plate in a line.

Sprinkle fried shallots on top of each quail as a garnish.

Serve.

Cider Braised Pork Butt, Smashed New Potatoes, Spicy Tomato Chutney

Cider Braised Pork Butt

- 2 cups chicken stock

- 1 (5 lb) pork butt, bone-in

- Salt and pepper, to taste

- 4 Tbsp olive oil

- 1 yellow onion, cut into medium-sized chunks

- 3 cloves garlic, peeled and crushed

- 1 Tbsp cumin

- 1 Tbsp coriander

- 3 cups apple cider

- 2 cups chicken stock

Preheat oven to 350°F.

Warm chicken stock in a saucepan over low heat. Set aside.

Season pork butt with freshly ground salt and pepper.

In a Dutch oven or heavy pot with a lid, add olive oil and pork butt.

Over medium heat, brown pork on all sides.

Remove pork and add onion, garlic, cumin, coriander, a pinch of salt, and a dash of pepper to Dutch oven.

Cook for 3–5 minutes until onions are soft.

Add cider to deglaze pot.

Return pork butt to pot and add stock.

Bring to a boil.

Remove from heat and place Dutch oven in preheated oven. Braise for 3 hours or until meat is fork tender.

Smashed New Potatoes

- 12 new potatoes

- 1 tsp salt

- ½ cup olive oil

Fill a large stock pot three-fourths of the way with water and bring to a boil.

Carefully add potatoes and salt.

Cook uncovered for 30 minutes, or until potatoes are fork tender.

Drain potatoes.

Place potatoes on a chopping board.

Using a fork, gently press down on the center of the potato until it smashes down but remains intact.

Drizzle potatoes with olive oil so that it seeps into the interior of the potatoes.

Place potatoes on a serving plate or platter and serve.

Spicy Tomato Chutney

- ½ cup red wine vinegar

- ¾ cup cider vinegar

- ¾ cup sugar

- 1 tsp salt

- 2 tsp mustard seeds

- ½ tsp fresh ground black pepper

- ½ tsp red pepper flakes

- ¾ cup chopped scallions, greens only, finely chopped

- 1 lb vine-ripened tomatoes, roughly chopped

- 1 red bell pepper, roughly chopped

In a medium saucepan, bring vinegars, sugar, salt, mustard seed, black pepper, and red pepper flakes to a boil, stirring occasionally.

Once boiling, add scallions, tomatoes, and bell pepper.

Simmer uncovered, stirring occasionally, for 1 hour or until thickened.

Mixture should reduce to approximately 1 ½ cups.

Allow to cool. Serve in small cups or bowls alongside potatoes.

Plum Pear Ricotta Bruschetta, Chocolate Fig Marmalade

- 4 slices Italian baguette, sliced into ½-inch diagonal slices

- 1 cup Nutella

- 1 cup fig marmalade or jam

- 1 cup ricotta cheese

- 1 ripe plum, sliced into ¼-inch vertical slices

- 1 ripe pear (Anjou or Bartlett), sliced into ¼-inch vertical slices

- 1 tsp salt

Place baguette slices onto a baking tray and lightly toast in the oven at 325°F for 15–20 minutes.

Remove baguette slices from the oven and let cool slightly.

Spread a thin layer of Nutella on each baguette slice.

Spread a thin layer of fig marmalade on top of the Nutella. Both spreads should almost melt into the bread.

Spread ¼ cup of the ricotta cheese across each baguette slice.

Top each slice with plum and pear slices, alternating between them.

Sprinkle ¼ teaspoon salt across the baguette slices.

Serve at room temperature.

Smoked Cod Carpaccio, Fried Capers, Grapefruit, Celery Fronds, Truffle Oil

- 1 lb smoked cod, sliced paper-thin

- 1 Tbsp olive oil

- 4 tsp capers

- 1 grapefruit, peeled, sections cut in half

- 2 stalks celery, fronds cut from stalks

- 2 tsp truffle oil

- 1 tsp freshly ground black pepper

Divide cod between 4 small salad plates, ¼ lb per plate.

In a small frying pan over medium heat, add olive oil until it sizzles, then add capers. Let cook 2 minutes. Shake pan. Let cook 2 minutes more, then shake pan again. Capers should look fried. Remove from heat and pour capers onto a paper towel to cool.

Place separated grapefruit pieces on top of cod.

Sprinkle capers over plate.

Finely dice the celery fronds and sprinkle evenly over the plates.

Drizzle truffle oil evenly over plates.

Season lightly with freshly ground black pepper.

Serve.

Assorted Cheeses, Membrillo, Torta De Aceite, Port

- 4 cheeses (a blue cheese like Roquefort, a hard cheese like Parmigiano-Reggiano, a soft cheese like Brie, and a crumbly cheese like goat cheese)

- Marcona almonds

- Torta de aceite (a Spanish olive oil biscuit)

- Membrillo (Spanish quince paste)

The evening is winding down, but no one is ready to go home.

The conversation is getting livelier, and the wine is only tasting better.

Serve a small platter of sweet and savory bites along with some port and bourbon.

Arrange on either a cheeseboard, a slate slab, or a ceramic tray.

Roasted Fennel, Spring Onion, Rucola, Buffalo Mozzarella, Pesto

- 1 fennel bulb, cut lengthwise into quarters, stalks trimmed to 3 inches

- 3 spring onions, halved lengthwise

- ½ cup olive oil

- salt and pepper to taste

- 1 cup basil pesto

- 1 large ball buffalo mozzarella, quartered

- 4 cups rucola greens

- ½ cup champagne vinaigrette

Place fennel and spring onions on a baking sheet and liberally toss with olive oil, salt, and pepper.

Bake at 425°F until soft, approximately 30 minutes.

On individual salad plates, build the salads.

Start by putting ¼ cup pesto onto the bottom of each plate, spreading it attractively.

Layer roasted fennel and spring onions.

Next add one fourth of the mozzarella to each plate.

Top salad with fresh rucola greens after tossing them lightly in vinaigrette. Season with salt and pepper.

Serve.

Cashmere Cocktail
Mulled Cider, Bourbon,
Sparkling Wine
Cinnamon

Cashmere & Caramel

...autumn in the air

Sweet Potato Blinis, Calvados Apples, Crème Fraîche, Caviar, Prosecco "Shot"

Butternut Squash Mascarpone Ravioli, Pine Nuts, Kale, Spicy Sage Brown Butter

Drunken Hen, Juniper, Rosemary Carrots, Garlic Celeriac Puree

Apple Hazelnut Tart, Spiced Crème, Mulled Cider

Serves 4

The Meal

Given that autumn is my favorite season, I really went all out with an atmosphere that felt decadent but homey at the same time. With only the candlelight in the room, it felt more intimate. Guests opened up faster, and laughter and storytelling became the theme of the table talk. Brooklyn experiences were exchanged ranging from food to shopping to bespoke live music venues and which neighborhoods had the best this or that.

As the final course was served, I made no efforts to clear the table. Everyone was so enjoying the evening that I just quietly slipped back to the kitchen to begin tidying up. It was so wonderful to hear the laughter and animated voices coming from the living room. Maybe it was the cocktail that made the guests a bit livelier this supper, or maybe it was just a moment in Brooklyn with a room full of strangers who found new friends.

The Theme

It could be argued that every season in New York is the best depending on who you ask. For me, it's all about autumn. The beautiful leaves are turning golden yellows, crimson reds, and pumpkin oranges. The air is still warm from the lingering summer sun, but there is just enough of a cool breeze coming off the water that says it's okay to pull out warm cashmere sweaters and scarves. We hear the crunch of leaves underfoot and smell more savory scents from passing restaurants. It's a wonderful new season for all of our senses.

The Setup

The table was set with dark red napkins and rich red roses in small bouquets down the entire table. Black wedding chairs surrounded the scene, and tons of tiny white votive candles in small glass vases lit up the table. A scattering of petite white pumpkins wrapped in caramel-colored ribbons reminded us of the autumn season. It felt lavish and decadent, yet cozy. I offered a welcome cocktail called "Cashmere." Who doesn't love the feel of cashmere? It evokes everything wonderful about autumn. Mulled cider, bourbon, and sparkling wine stirred with a cinnamon stick set the stage for the wonderful night ahead.

Over a bed of Celeriac

Warm Apple Hazelnut Tart
With Fresh Cream & Mulled
Cider

Sweet Potato Blinis, Calvados Apples, Crème Fraîche, Caviar, Prosecco "Shot"

- 3 Tbsp all-purpose flour
- 2 Tbsp buckwheat flour
- ½ sweet potato, cooked, peeled, and pureed
- 1 tsp sugar
- ⅛ tsp baking soda
- 1 tsp kosher salt
- ¼ cup whole milk
- 1 large egg, separated
- 3 Tbsp melted unsalted butter, divided
- 3 Tbsp butter
- 2 Fuji or Gala apples, peeled, cored, and cut into 1-inch pieces
- ½ cup calvados
- 4 Tbsp crème fraîche
- 4 Tbsp black caviar, osetra
- 2 cups prosecco, chilled

In a bowl, whisk together flours, potato, sugar, baking soda, and salt.

Whisk in milk and egg yolk.

In separate bowl, whisk egg white until soft peaks form.

Gently fold egg white into batter until just combined.

Fold 2 tablespoons melted butter into batter and stir gently.

In a cast iron or non-stick skillet, heat ½ tablespoon butter over medium heat.

In batches, spoon 1 tablespoon batter into the skillet, and cook until bubbly and dry on top, approximately 1 minute.

Flip blini and cook until golden brown on bottom.

Transfer to a serving platter until all are cooked.

In a sauté pan, add apples and 1 tablespoon butter over medium heat.

Cook until apples are soft. Add calvados and cook on high heat for 3–5 minutes.

To plate, layer sautéed apples on top of blini.

Top apples with 1 tablespoon crème fraiche and 1 tablespoon caviar.

Fill small juice or Moroccan tea glasses with chilled prosecco to be served alongside the dish.

Serve.

Butternut Squash Mascarpone Ravioli, Pine Nuts, Kale, Spicy Sage Brown Butter

- 1 whole butternut squash

- 3 Tbsp olive oil

- 1 tsp nutmeg

- 1 cup mascarpone cheese

- 3 cups all-purpose flour

- 3 tsp salt, divided

- 5 eggs, divided

- 1 tsp black pepper

- 1 cup pine nuts

- 2 cups kale, washed

- 2 sticks unsalted butter

- 1 Tbsp garlic, minced

- 4 sage leaves, roughly chopped

- 1 tsp red pepper flakes

- 1 cup Parmigiano-Reggiano shavings

Cut squash in half from top to bottom.

Remove seeds.

Brush both halves of squash with olive oil.

Sprinkle nutmeg across both halves.

Roast at 350°F for 40 minutes, or until soft.

Spoon squash out of shell and into a blender.

Add mascarpone.

Puree until smooth.

Set aside.

In a stand mixer with a dough hook, combine flour and salt. Add 4 eggs, one at a time, and continue to mix. Drizzle in olive oil and continue to mix until a ball forms.

Spread a little flour on the counter, and knead dough until smooth and elastic. Wrap in plastic wrap, and let dough rest for 30 minutes.

Cut the ball in half. Dust counter with flour and form each half into a rectangle. Feed dough through a pasta machine 2–3 times at widest setting, then 2–3 times at the narrowest setting.

No pasta machine? No worries.

The Brooklyn Suppers

Use a rolling pin to get the dough to the same thinness, approximately ⅛-inch thick.

Dust dough with flour and lay it on the counter.

Brush dough with 1 whisked egg yolk.

Place a few tablespoons of cooled squash filling 2 inches apart on one half of pasta sheet, lengthwise.

Lay other half of rolled dough over the filling.

Gently press out any air pockets around each mound with fingers and create a seal.

Using a crimper tool, cut each pillow into squares. (Substitution would be a pizza cutter and crimp edges with a fork.)

Be sure they are well sealed.

Cook ravioli in boiling salted water for 12 minutes or until ravioli float to the top.

Remove cooked raviolis with a slotted spoon.

Place on a clean dry platter.

In a dry sauté pan over medium heat, add pine nuts.

Add 1 teaspoon salt.

Toss nuts every few minutes as they lightly brown.

Remove and place on a paper towel when browned and glistening.

In a sauté pan, add 1 tablespoon olive oil.

Bring to a sizzle and add kale plus 1 tablespoon of water.

Sauté until wilted, 5 minutes.

Set aside.

In a sauce pan, melt butter.

Add garlic, sage, red pepper flakes, and sautéed kale.

Cook over medium heat for 8 minutes, stirring occasionally.

Remove from heat and add salt and pepper to taste.

Place 3 raviolis on each plate.

Spoon kale and sage brown butter sauce over raviolis, and garnish with toasted pine nuts and Parmigiano-Reggiano shavings.

Serve.

Drunken Hen, Juniper, Rosemary Carrots, Garlic Celeriac Puree

Drunken Hen

- 2 Cornish game hens, halved
- 1 yellow onion, coarsely chopped
- 4 Tbsp chopped garlic
- 2 carrots, coarsely chopped
- 1 celery stalk, coarsely chopped
- ½ cup juniper berries, dried
- 4 sprigs fresh thyme
- Fresh ground salt and pepper
- 1 bottle dry white wine (pinot grigio)
- 1 Tbsp olive oil
- 1 bouquet garni (fresh rosemary, sage, and thyme tied with kitchen string into a little bundle)
- 1 Tbsp flour

Rinse and dry hens. Set aside.

In a large bowl, add onion, garlic, carrots, celery, juniper, thyme, salt, pepper, and three-fourths of the bottle of white wine.

Add hens to the bowl and marinate 6 hours.

Heat olive oil in a deep skillet and add bouquet garni.

Add the well-drained hens and brown on all sides over medium-high heat.

When hens are browned, add flour to the pan.

Turn hens and add remaining white wine.

Cover and let cook over low heat until chicken is tender and cooked through, approximately 20 minutes.

Remove from heat and let rest 5 minutes.

Rosemary Carrots

4 whole carrots with leaves still on*

½ cup olive oil

4 springs fresh rosemary

Salt and pepper, to taste

Preheat oven to 375°F.

Rinse and pat carrots dry. Remove carrot tops with leaves. Set aside.

In a roasting pan, add carrots (whole) with olive oil and toss.

Finely chop rosemary after removing stems. Add rosemary to pan.

Season lightly with salt and pepper.

Toss to incorporate.

Roast for 35–40 minutes until soft when pierced with a fork.

*Up your game by seeking out organic rainbow carrots, which are a mixed assortment of red, white, purple, and orange carrots. They not only add great color to the dish, but are delicious as well.

Garlic Celeriac Puree

- 4 celeriac (celery root), peeled and quartered

- 1 tsp salt

- 2 cloves garlic, peeled

- 1 Tbsp olive oil

- ½ cup heavy cream

Bring 4 cups of water to a boil in a large pot.

Add celeriac, salt, and garlic.

Boil until celeriac is fork tender (same as a potato).

Remove from heat and drain in a colander.

Once drained, transfer to a mixing bowl or even back into the pot.

Add olive oil and heavy cream. With a hand held blender, puree until smooth.

Season with salt and pepper.

Serve.

Apple Hazelnut Tart, Spiced Crème, Mulled Cider

Dough

- 2 cups all-purpose flour

- 1 tsp kosher salt

- ½ cup finely chopped hazelnuts

- 1 Tbsp sugar

- 1½ sticks cold unsalted butter, diced

- ½ cup cold water

In a food processor, add flour, salt, hazelnuts, and sugar and combine well.

Add butter and pulse 10 times or until butter is in small pieces.

With food processor running, slowly add cold water down the feed tube.

Dough should come together as a ball.

Remove dough ball and place on a floured surface and knead into the shape of a ball.

Wrap in plastic wrap and refrigerate for 1 hour.

The Brooklyn Suppers

Filling

- 4 apples (Gala or Granny Smith are best)
- ½ cup sugar
- 4 Tbsp cold unsalted butter, diced
- ½ cup apple jelly
- 2 Tbsp water

While the pastry is in the refrigerator, prepare the apples.

Peel apples.

Cut in half and remove stems and cores.

Slice apples lengthwise (top to bottom) into ¼-inch slices.

Sprinkle with 1 tablespoon sugar.

Toss to incorporate.

Preheat oven to 400°F.

Line a sheet pan with parchment paper.

Roll out dough to fit the sheet pan.

Trim edges for a clean rectangular shape.

Place apples on pastry in slightly overlapping rows.

Keep making rows until pastry is covered.

Leave a small outer edge around tart.

Sprinkle tart evenly with ½ cup sugar.

Place diced butter pieces evenly across pastry.

Bake 45 minutes until pastry edges are brown. Keep watch during cooking to watch for bubbling. If tart bubbles, just poke it with a fork or knife to deflate.

Remove cooked pastry from the oven. Let cool.

Warm jelly, either in pan or microwave, and brush the top of the pastry to glaze.

With a pizza cutter, slice pastry into equal-sized squares or rectangles.

Use a spatula to remove tart slices and place on serving plates or dishes.

Topping

- 2 cups whipping cream
- 1 tsp sugar
- 1 tsp nutmeg
- 1 tsp cinnamon

In a mixing bowl, add whipping cream, sugar, nutmeg, and cinnamon.

Using a whisk, blend until cream stiffens with soft peaks.

Add a dollop of fresh cream to each tart.

Serve with a warm cup of mulled apple cider, maybe even spiked with bourbon!

QUWAT UL ISLAM MASJID AND IRON PILLAR, DELHI (INDIA).

once upon a time...

Bohemian Bourgeois

Moules, Thai Style

Butterleaf, Duck Lardons, Quail Egg Salad

**Grilled Hen of the Woods,
Black Sesame, Balsamic**

**Pork Rillettes, Wheat Baguette, Cornichon,
Pickled Carrot, Grain Mustard**

**Rosemary Rib Roast, Porcini Au Jus,
Petatou**

**Gingerbread Pumpkin Roll,
Salted Caramel Sauce**

Serves 4

The Meal

The menu was a huge undertaking, and I had to start a week early with some of the dishes, like the rillettes. I couldn't have been prouder at the success of the courses in the end.

Equally as successful was the mood of the table during this supper. So much more laughter and joking and elevated voices than at any other supper. Everyone embraced the theme and in the light of the next day, while cleaning up, I found so many wonderful notes and drawings. Notes to the other guests without them knowing. Notes to the chef in thanks of bringing together strangers and creating new friends. Notes about the success of the food and notes to never stop what I was doing as it was creating community.

The Theme

Bohemian Bourgeois was one of my favorite and most challenging themes, both in the kitchen and in setting the table. I wanted the food to be authentic French cuisine, but that was not really in my culinary vernacular. I wanted the table to be a representation of the Bohemian movement and lifestyle found among the artists, writers, and creators of nineteenth century France. I hoped that the theme would evoke interesting conversations that would differ from the normal small talk. I hoped that the food would spark even more excitement, as they weren't your everyday dishes, even in Brooklyn.

The Setup

I set the table with Moroccan tea glasses filled with pencils, markers, and crayons. Small turquoise votives lit the table and were the only source of light in the room. I scattered vintage postcards and tiny notebooks down the table to encourage guests to write a note, draw a picture, or just be creative. I typed little quotes or feelings or expressions on paper and scattered them across the table as well. The napkins were ones I had purchased in India and featured a block-printed design that felt loud and opinionated. I wanted to get the conversation going just like in the cafes in Paris.

Moules, Thai Style

- 1 Tbsp high-quality vegetable oil

- 2 Tbsp garlic, finely chopped

- 2 stalks lemongrass, finely chopped

- 1 Tbsp galangal, peeled and
  finely chopped

- 2 lb very fresh mussels, cleaned
  under cold running water and
  debearded (remove any tendrils)*

- 1 cup white wine (pinot grigio
  preferred)

- 1 cup coconut milk

- ½ cup Thai basil,
  roughly chopped

*Remove any mussels that are not tightly
closed or cracked.*

In a stock pot, warm oil. Add garlic, lemongrass, and galangal.

Stir a few times over 5 minutes until sautéed.

Add mussels, tossing ingredients together.

Add wine and coconut milk, tossing again, and cover with lid.

When mussels are open, remove from heat.

In single bowls or one larger serving dish, ladle out contents.

Garnish with basil.

Serve.

Butterleaf, Duck Lardons, Quail Egg Salad

- 2 cups duck lardons (can substitute with pancetta lardons)

- 1 Tbsp olive oil, divided

- 4 quail eggs (buy 6 in case of error)

- 1 tsp Dijon mustard

- 1 Tbsp champagne vinegar

- Salt and pepper to taste

- 1 head butterleaf lettuce

- 2 Tbsp goat cheese, crumbled

In a small sauté pan, cook duck lardons in 1 teaspoon olive oil until crispy.

In same pan, fry each quail egg without adding any more oil.

Combine Dijon, remaining olive oil, vinegar, and salt and pepper to taste and shake until all flavors are melded into a dressing.

Place 1–2 butterleaf lettuce leaves on each plate.

Top with an egg and sprinkle with lardons and cheese.

Dress with vinaigrette.

Season with salt and pepper.

Serve.

Grilled Hen of the Woods, Black Sesame, Balsamic

- 1 Tbsp black sesame seeds

- 1 Tbsp olive oil

- 1 Tbsp butter

- 2 tsp fresh thyme, finely chopped

- 2 shallots, finely chopped

- 2 cloves garlic, finely chopped

- 2 Tbsp balsamic vinegar

- 2 cups fresh spinach leaves

- 2 large hen of the woods mushroom clusters, cleaned with soft cloth of any dirt and halved

Sauté black sesame seeds in a sauté pan until lightly toasted.

Remove from heat and set aside in small bowl.

Add olive oil and heat over medium heat.

Add butter, thyme, shallots, garlic, vinegar, and spinach.

Sauté until shallots and garlic are soft.

Add mushrooms and sauté for 2–3 minutes, turning once in the pan.

Remove mushrooms from pan, and add black sesame seeds to the pan.

Plate mushrooms.

Pour 1 tablespoon of pan sauce over mushrooms.

Serve.

Pork Rillettes, Wheat Baguette, Cornichon, Pickled Carrot, Grain Mustard

- 2 lb pork belly, cut into 2-inch cubes

- 1 lb pork shoulder, cut into 2-inch cubes

- 4 cups water

- 1 bouquet garni (fresh rosemary, sage, and thyme tied with kitchen string into a little bundle)

- 1 tsp salt

- 1 tsp black pepper

- 1 lb pork fat, cut into ¼-inch thick slices

In a heavy-bottomed pan, add pork belly, pork shoulder, water, and bouquet garni.

Cover and cook over low heat for approximately 6 hours.

Stir occasionally.

Add salt and pepper.

Let meat cool and when able to be handled, transfer to a work surface or large bowl.

Using a fork, shred meat.

Do not butcher it.

Be sure to pull it apart as it naturally falls, similar to BBQ.

Divide the mixture into small containers, 4–6 ounces each.

Top completely with slices of pork fat.

Wrap containers in plastic wrap, sealing containers tightly.

Refrigerate for 3 days. Yes, 3 days.

Remove and place tastefully onto serving plates or a platter.

You can use a biscuit cutter or even the rim of glass to form the rillettes into clean, round uniform shapes.

Garnish with a small thyme or rosemary cutting across the top.

Serve rillettes with wheat baguette slices, cornichons, pickled carrots (yes, you can use store-bought), and a nice, quality grain mustard.

Keep refrigerated (if there are any leftovers) for no longer than a week.

Rosemary Rib Roast, Porcini Au Jus, Petatou

Rosemary Rib Roast

- 1 standing rib roast of beef
  (approximately 6 lb)

- 4 cloves garlic, thinly slivered

- Salt and pepper

- 2 Tbsp rosemary, finely chopped

Preheat oven to 450°F.

With a paring knife, cut small slits into the roast.

Insert garlic slivers into the slits.

Season entire roast with freshly ground salt, pepper, and rosemary.

Place roast on the rack of a roasting pan.

Cook for 25 minutes, then reduce heat to 350°F.

Continue cooking for another hour and a half until the internal temperature reads 140°F.

Remove from oven, and let rest at least 15 minutes.

While the meat is resting, prepare the porcini jus.

The Brooklyn Suppers

Porcini Jus

- 3 Tbsp unsalted butter
- 1 shallot, finely chopped
- 2 cloves garlic, thinly sliced
- ¼ cup red wine
- 1 quart beef stock
- ¼ cup sherry vinegar
- 4 thyme sprigs
- 1 cup dried porcini, ground into powder

In a saucepan, melt butter.

Add shallot and garlic, and cook until browned.

Add wine and boil for 2 minutes.

Add stock, vinegar, and thyme.

Bring to a boil.

Simmer until reduced to 2 ½ cups, approximately 15 minutes.

Strain sauce and return to pan.

Whisk in porcini powder and simmer for 2 minutes.

Remove from heat and cover for 5 minutes.

Carve the roast into 1-inch thick slices.

Pour 2–3 tablespoons porcini jus over each slice.

Petatou (Potato Tart)

- 1½ lb Yukon gold potatoes
- 1 pinch each salt and pepper
- 1 cup heavy cream
- 1 egg yolk
- 1 cup olive oil
- ⅓ cup balsamic vinegar
- 3 shallots, finely chopped
- 1 Tbsp fresh chopped basil
- 1 Tbsp fresh chopped thyme
- 1 Tbsp fresh chopped Italian parsley
- 10 oz goat cheese log, cut into ½-inch rounds

Boil potatoes in salted water until tender.

Drain, peel, and cut potatoes into ½-inch rounds.

Put potatoes in a bowl with salt and pepper to taste.

In a separate bowl, whip cream until peaks form, then add egg yolk to bowl. Whisk in olive oil. Pour the cream mixture into potatoes, reserving one-third of the mixture.

In a separate bowl, whisk vinegar, shallots, and half of the chopped herbs.

Put remaining half of herbs in with potatoes along with all but 1 tablespoon of vinegar and herb mixture.

Either in individual ramekins or in metal rings on a cookie sheet, place potatoes in a small round shape about 1-inch high.

Preheat oven to 350°F.

Top each round with a tablespoon of the remaining cream mixture and the goat cheese rounds to top the cream.

Place in oven for 5–7 minutes to brown tops of the potatoes.

Remove from oven and top each with a teaspoon or so of the remaining herb mixture.

The Brooklyn Suppers

Gingerbread Pumpkin Roll, Salted Caramel Sauce

- 3 large eggs
- ½ cup sugar
- ½ cup dark molasses
- ⅔ cup canned pumpkin
- 1 tsp lemon juice
- ¾ cup all-purpose flour
- 1 tsp ground ginger
- 2 tsp ground salt
- 1 tsp baking powder
- 1 tsp ground cinnamon
- 2 cups pecans, finely chopped, divided
- 1 ½ cups confectioners' sugar
- 6 oz cream cheese, room temperature
- 1 stick unsalted butter, room temperature
- ½ tsp vanilla extract
- 12 pieces caramel candies
- ½ tsp salt

Preheat oven to 350°F.

Lightly grease and dust a sheet pan with flour.

Using an electric mixer, beat eggs, sugar, molasses, pumpkin, and lemon juice until smooth.

Sift together flour, ginger, salt, baking powder, and cinnamon.

Combine sifted ingredients with wet ingredients.

Batter should be smooth and creamy.

Spread batter on the prepared sheet pan.

Sprinkle dough evenly with 1 cup chopped pecans.

Bake 15 minutes, checking after 12 minutes to see if a toothpick comes out clean; if so, remove.

Let cool 5 minutes and invert onto a wire rack.

Lay out a clean kitchen or tea towel and dust with confectioners' sugar.

Place warm cake on the towel.

Fold the sides of the towel over the cake.

Roll cake up in the towel and cool for 45 minutes.

Using an electric mixer, combine confectioners' sugar, cream cheese, butter, and vanilla.

Beat until smooth.

Carefully unroll cooled cake and spread cream cheese mixture across the cake surface evenly.

Roll cake up again, without the towel, ending with seam on the bottom.

Gently place on a serving platter and dust with confectioners' sugar.

In a small saucepan, melt the caramel candies with salt.

Spread 1 tablespoon caramel sauce on serving plates.

Cut roll into 1-inch rounds and place flat on plates.

Sprinkle remaining pecan pieces across the top.

Serve.

Cinema & Supper

**Ratatouille Tart, Tomato Jam,
Ricotta, Microgreens**

Lobster, Mango, Beet, Fennel, Mint Vinaigrette

Shanghai-Style Sea Bass, Chanterelles, Spinach, Chili Ponzu Broth

Linguini with Grandma's Gravy

Mesquite Grilled Quail, Red Rose Sauce

Berries and Balsamic Eton Mess Bar

Serves 4

The Meal

What an enchanting evening we had! Prior to each course being served, I played a scene of the film represented by that course. I projected the scene onto an eight-foot screen hung from my brownstone ceiling. The clip set the tone for the dish and the conversations. Some were happy memories from childhood like *Hook*, some created more sober conversations, like *Like Water for Chocolate* and *Eat Drink Man Woman*. There was laughter for *Goodfellas* and *Ratatouille*. The conversations around the table moved from cinema to music to Broadway to off-Broadway. Guests lingered yet again. A mention of a small, quaint bar around the corner rallied the guests. For the first time since hosting the suppers, I joined my guests for a nightcap up the street. The mood was too high to say no and well, the dishes will always be there when I get home!

The Theme

While traveling in China for work, I stumbled across a beautiful film one night while tucked into my hotel bed and channel surfing. It was called *Eat Drink Man Woman*. Yes, it was subtitled, but the film itself had very little conversation. It was more about the quietness and beauty of cooking—the immersion of one's self into preparing food for loved ones. It's a beautiful film, and it inspired me to create a supper with each course based on a film. Not just any film. A film that shared a story about food and about humankind. I called it "Cinema & Supper: An Around-the-World Taste of Six Cultures through Six Inspired Movie Moments." The movies I chose were *Ratatouille*, *Annie Hall*, *Eat Drink Man Woman*, *Goodfellas*, *Like Water for Chocolate*, and *Hook*.

The Setup

Since I created this supper theme while in China, I gathered some table setting supplies from the outdoor markets while still there: little silk drawstring bags all in unique colors for the takeaway "crack candy," beautiful black chopsticks for the linguini, and bamboo spoons for the eton mess dessert. Since it was the beginning of spring in Brooklyn, I put delicate baby's breath flowers nestled into wheat grass in small rectangular glass vases. I created a separate dessert table to really showcase the eton mess. Colorful meringues in tons of soft pink, mocha, and mint were crumbled over spiced whipped cream, balsamic marinated strawberries, and chopped pecans.

Ratatouille Tart, Tomato Jam, Ricotta, Microgreens

Film: *Ratatouille*

Ratatouille Tart

- 3 cups all-purpose flour
- 1 ½ sticks cold unsalted butter, cut into ½-inch pieces
- 3 Tbsp extra virgin olive oil
- 4 Tbsp cold water
- 1 zucchini
- 1 yellow squash
- 6 plum tomatoes
- 1 cup Parmesan cheese, grated
- ½ cup fresh basil, finely chopped
- 2 Tbsp roasted garlic
- Pinch each salt and pepper
- 1 cup fresh ricotta cheese
- 1 cup microgreens

Combine flour and butter in a bowl and blend until smooth. Add olive oil and water, and combine until dough has formed. Make it into a ball, wrap in plastic wrap, and chill for 30 minutes in the refrigerator.

Preheat oven to 350°F.

Remove the dough from refrigerator, remove the plastic wrap, and spread it evenly into an oiled tart pan, being sure to push it well into the sides so that it creates the tart's edges.

Bake for 25 minutes until cooked through and lightly browned.

While tart shell cooks, use a mandolin to slice zucchini, squash, and tomatoes into ⅛-inch slices.

Remove tart from oven.

Sprinkle Parmesan, basil, and roasted garlic on the bottom of the tart.

Layer vegetables in a circular pattern around tart, starting at the outside and moving in.

Overlap vegetable circles two-thirds over the next, and alternate each of the three vegetables as you layer.

Continue to layer in overlapping circles toward the center of the tart.

When you reach the middle, layer one single vegetable round in the center.

Drizzle a little olive oil over the tart and season with salt and pepper.

Return to oven and cook 25 minutes.

Remove and cool.

When serving, cut the tart as you would a pie.

Garnish with a scoop of fresh ricotta and microgreens.

Serve tomato jam on the side.

Tomato Jam

- 2 lb plum tomatoes, cored and cut into 1-inch pieces
- 2 Tbsp apple cider vinegar
- ½ cup dark brown sugar
- 1 Tbsp fresh ginger, peeled and grated
- 1 tsp salt
- ½ tsp cumin
- ¼ tsp smoked paprika
- ¼ tsp red pepper flakes

In a heavy-bottomed pan, combine all ingredients.

Bring to a boil over medium heat, stirring often.

Simmer until thickened, approximately 2 hours, stirring every now and then.

Jam is done when it does not return to center when stirred.

Refrigerate until cool.

Will keep for 10 days in refrigerator.

Lobster, Mango, Beet, Fennel, Mint Vinaigrette

Film: *Annie Hall*

- 2 Tbsp salt

- 1 Tbsp white vinegar

- 2 fresh lobster tails

- 1 stick cold unsalted butter, cut into small pieces

- 1 Tbsp fresh lemon juice

- 1 fresh rosemary sprig, approximately 3 inches long

- 2 yellow beets

- 1 Tbsp olive oil

- 1 Tbsp fresh mint, finely chopped

- 1 Tbsp red wine vinegar

- 1 tsp fresh garlic, minced

- 1 tsp Dijon mustard

- 1 head fennel, cleaned, outer layer removed and shaved with a grater into thin strips

- 1 mango, halved, pit removed, and scored into ½-inch cubes

Bring a large pot of water to boil. Add salt and white vinegar to water.

Add lobster tails and cook 3 minutes.

Remove tails from water and let cool.

Remove outer shell and cut lobster into 1-inch pieces.

In a saucepan over low heat, add butter, lemon juice, and rosemary sprig.

Bring to a soft boil and submerge lobster meat.

Poach until opaque, about 3 minutes.

Remove from heat. Take lobster meat out and set aside.

Using a peeler, remove outer layer of yellow beets, cut into 1-inch pieces, and place on a roasting pan. Toss with olive oil and bake in a 350°F oven. Roast beets until tender, approximately 30 minutes.

In a separate bowl, whisk together 3 tablespoons poaching liquid, mint, olive oil, red wine vinegar, garlic, and Dijon.

On salad plates, place ½ cup fresh lobster meat, top with beets, fresh mango, and shaved fennel.

Dress with vinaigrette.

Serve.

Shanghai-Styled Sea Bass, Chanterelles, Spinach, Chili Ponzu Broth

Film: *Eat Drink Man Woman*

- 1 lb fresh sea bass
- 4 cups fish stock
- 1 cup chili ponzu sauce
- 2 cups fresh chanterelle mushrooms
- 4 cups fresh spinach

Rinse fish and pat dry.

Set aside on clean plate.

In a deep sauté pan, add fish stock and ponzu sauce, cook over medium heat. Do not let it boil.

Add sea bass, making sure it is fully submerged.

Cook for 5 minutes.

Add mushrooms and spinach.

Continue cooking until fish is tender and almost falling apart, approximately 15 minutes total cooking time.

In shallow bowls, spoon one-fourth of spinach mixture.

Top with one-fourth of the fish.

Add one-fourth of the mushrooms over the top of the fish.

Spoon broth over the fish until it covers the spinach.

Serve.

Linguini with Grandma's Gravy

Film: *Goodfellas*

In memory of my Nonna Antonelli

Gravy

- 10 cloves of garlic, peeled
- ¼ cup olive oil
- 1 Tbsp crushed red pepper
- 4 16-oz cans whole peeled tomatoes
- 1 small carrot
- Salt and pepper to taste

In paper-thin slices, cut all of the garlic lengthwise.

Over low heat in a stock pot, add the olive oil and garlic.

Remove from heat when garlic is very lightly browned; it will be burned and bitter if it cooks too much.

Turn off heat and add red pepper.

Stir to combine.

Add whole tomatoes and whole carrot.

Cook for 45 minutes over low heat.

Stir periodically.

Remove from heat and remove carrot.

Puree tomatoes with a hand blender.

Pour through a strainer.

Season to taste with salt and pepper.

Linguini

- 1 lb store-bought fresh linguini; use dry pasta if fresh cannot be found
- 1 tsp salt
- ½ cup fresh basil, chiffoned
- 1 cup shaved Parmigiano-Reggiano cheese

Once pasta sauce has been made, start a large pot of boiling water, approximately 6 quarts.

Add 1 tsp salt and pasta.

Cook approximately 2–3 minutes until al dente.

Remove and strain in a colander.

To plate, place a big forkful (1 cup) of linguini in the bottom of a shallow pasta bowl.

Top linguini with 1 cup gravy.

Garnish with 1 teaspoon fresh basil and 1 tablespoon shaved Parmigiano-Reggiano.

Optional—add fresh ground black pepper over top.

Serve.

Mesquite Grilled Quail, Red Rose Sauce

Film: *Like Water for Chocolate*

Red Rose Sauce

- 3 cups water
- 12 fresh chestnuts
- 2 Tbsp butter
- 2 cloves garlic, minced
- ½ tsp anise seed
- 12 red roses, open blooms, petals only
- 1 red cactus fruit, peeled and skinned
- 2 Tbsp honey
- Salt and pepper to taste

Bring water to a boil.

Using a small knife, make an X at the flat ends of each chestnut.

Toast chestnuts in a hot pan for 5 minutes.

When shells open, add chestnuts to the boiling water and cook for 15 minutes.

Drain and allow nuts to cool, then peel.

In a large saucepan, melt butter.

Add garlic and anise seed and cook for 5 minutes.

Remove from heat.

Put the rose petals and cactus fruit in a blender.

Puree until smooth.

Add cooked chestnuts and 1 cup of water.

Puree until smooth.

Reheat butter mixture and add to rose puree.

Simmer for 5 minutes, then add honey and salt and pepper to taste.

Pour sauce through a strainer into a clean pan.

Sauce can remain over very low heat while quail are grilling.

Quail

- 8 semi-boneless quail
- 2 Tbsp mesquite smoke powder
- 1 Tbsp olive oil

Rinse quail and pat dry.

Combine mesquite smoke powder with 2 tablespoons olive oil.

Stir to combine.

Rub spice mixture all over quail.

Grill quail over medium heat until cooked, approximately 8–10 minutes, turning once.

Remove from heat and let rest.

Pour ½ cup rose sauce over each dinner plate and place quail in the middle.

Serve.

Berries and Balsamic Eton Mess Bar

Film: *Hook*

"Laughter is timeless…imagination has no age…dreams are forever."—Tinkerbell

Traditionally, eton mess is an English dessert layering strawberries, broken meringues, and whipped cream in a clear parfait glass or bowl. For this supper, we have presented all the ingredients on a buffet table, allowing guests to build their perfect eton mess.

My recipe includes a few revisions to the classic recipe.

- 2 pints fresh strawberries
- 2 pints blackberries
- 2 pints blueberries
- 1 cup balsamic vinegar
- 1 dozen pink meringues
- 1 dozen white meringues
- 1 dozen tan meringues
- 2 cups pecans, roughly chopped
- 4 cups fresh whipped cream
- 1 bottle prosecco

Marinate berries in balsamic vinegar for an hour.

Spice up the whipped cream by folding in nutmeg and cinnamon.

Use colorful meringues, not just white ones.

Sprinkle in chopped pecans as an extra layer and for crunch.

Serve by adding ¼ cup of prosecco to the bottom of each glass, and you will end up with a delicious last bite!

Posh Picnic

Roasted Red Radish, Red Onion, Herbed Goat Cheese Bruschetta

Zucchini Ribbons, Prosciutto, Champagne Vinaigrette

Oven-Fried Chicken, Posh Potato Salad

Strawberry Balsamic and Blueberry Thyme Homemade Hand Pies

**Avocado, Pecan, Cranberry,
Black Basmati Pilaf**

Serves 4

The Meal

Guests arrived just at dusk and were served a glass of prosecco as they casually gathered in the meadow. As the prosecco was topped off, they took their seats at the long dining tables with no assigned seating. Strangers became new friends in their own community, some living only down the street from one another. There was a lot of talk of local events, a bit of gossip, farming, and how the gardens are growing. The sun set and the plates were emptied. A local business owner broke out a guitar and was shortly joined by a violin and a harmonica. We spent the next hour enjoying the sounds of nature, musical instruments, and song.

The Theme

The word was getting out about my suppers from social media posts. My mother owned and ran a glamping farm in the Georgia mountains, and she asked me to host a supper on her farm using the fresh, organic local produce, meat, and dairy found in the countryside. So, I packed the car and Sula, and I headed down South. The dinner was to be served under a large custom-designed tent placed on a wooden platform. Guests would dine alfresco at sunset overlooking a large meadow and the forest. I wanted to bring the outdoors in by having the guests sit at long harvest tables with all the comforts of dining indoors. My first truly farm-to-table event was a great success and somehow I knew I would be back.

The Setup

I wanted the outdoor event to be just as luxurious and comfortable as any posh restaurant. Crystal chandeliers hung overhead making the wine glasses and china twinkle in the light. Silver cutlery, linen tablecloths, fine china plates, and fresh-from-the-garden flower arrangements adorned the table. Italian wedding lights were strung around the platform railings, and the music of the night was brought to us by crickets chirping, birds tweeting, and the occasional chicken clucking from the coop just nearby.

Roasted Red Radish, Red Onion, Herbed Goat Cheese Bruschetta

- 1 French baguette, sliced into ½-inch rounds (two slices per person)

- 1 cup herbed goat cheese (you can mix freshly chopped fine herbs directly into the cheese or buy an already herbed goat cheese from the market)

- 8 red radishes, rinsed and sliced into ¼-inch rounds

- 1 large red onion, sliced into ¼-inch thick rounds

- 2 Tbsp olive oil

Lightly brush the baguette slices with olive oil and toast them under the broiler.

Place baguette slices on a serving platter.

Spread 1 tsp of goat cheese across each baguette slice.

Place radish and onion slices on a cookie sheet and toss with olive oil until coated.

Roast in the oven for 20 minutes at 400°F or until soft.

Top baguette slices with a few radishes and a few onions.

Zucchini Ribbons, Prosciutto, Champagne Vinaigrette

- 4 wooden skewers
- 1 zucchini, thinly shaved using a peeler
- 8 paper-thin slices prosciutto
- ¼ cup olive oil
- ¼ cup champagne vinegar
- 1 tsp garlic, finely chopped
- 2 tsp fresh basil, finely chopped
- 2 tsp fresh thyme, finely chopped
- 1 tsp Dijon mustard
- 1 tsp salt
- 1 tsp pepper

Soak skewers in warm water for 15 minutes, pat dry.

On a clean plate, layer zucchini slices on top of prosciutto slices until you have 12 layered sheets.

Gently weave one sheet onto the top of the skewer in a back and forth pattern.

Then slide the sheet down the skewer to the bottom third.

Repeat until you have 3 sheets woven onto the skewer.

Repeat these steps until you have 4 full skewers.

In a mixing bowl, combine olive oil, vinegar, garlic, basil, thyme, Dijon, and salt and pepper.

Whisk until blended into a light vinaigrette.

Brush or drizzle vinaigrette over skewers.

The Brooklyn Suppers

Oven-Fried Chicken, Posh Potato Salad

Oven-Fried Chicken

- 4 boneless chicken breasts
- 2 cups buttermilk
- 2 cups breadcrumbs, plain and fine
- 1 Tbsp fresh rosemary, finely chopped
- 1 cup olive oil

Rinse chicken breasts and pat dry.

Place buttermilk and breadcrumbs in separate bowls.

Add rosemary to the breadcrumb bowl and toss.

Dredge chicken breasts first in buttermilk, shaking off any excess, then in the breadcrumbs. Set the breaded chicken on a clean plate. Repeat for all breasts.

Warm olive oil in a frying pan until just sizzling.

Carefully set chicken breasts in pan.

Cook on each side for 10 minutes, making sure the exterior crisps up but does not burn. You want a golden brown, crunchy exterior and a tender, moist interior.

Remove from heat and let rest.

Posh Potato Salad

- 2 tsp salt
- 12 red bliss potatoes
- 5 strips bacon, cooked
- 1 tsp paprika
- 2 green onions, thinly sliced
- ½ cup plus 1 Tbsp fresh chopped cilantro, divided
- 1 tsp garlic salt
- 2 tsp black pepper, fresh ground
- 2 Tbsp olive oil
- 1 Tbsp mayonnaise
- 1 Tbsp red wine vinegar
- 2 tsp Dijon mustard
- ½ cup Parmigiano-Reggiano cheese, grated

Bring a pot of water to boil.

Add salt.

Add potatoes to the pot. Boil until cooked through, approximately 20 minutes.

Drain, rinse, and place the potatoes in large mixing bowl.

Crumble in bacon into a bowl. Add paprika, green onions, and 1 tablespoon cilantro.

In a small mixing bowl, add garlic salt, black pepper, olive oil, mayonnaise, vinegar, and mustard.

Whisk until blended into a vinaigrette.

Pour vinaigrette over potatoes.

Add Parmigiano-Reggiano cheese and rest of cilantro.

Toss and serve with oven-fried chicken.

Strawberry Balsamic and Blueberry Thyme Homemade Hand Pies

Strawberry Balsamic Filling

- 1 quart whole strawberries
- ½ cup balsamic vinegar
- 2 tsp black pepper
- 1 tsp salt

Cut strawberries into quarters.

Place in a bowl and add vinegar.

Add salt and pepper.

Toss together, let sit.

Blueberry Thyme Filling

- 1 quart blueberries
- 1 Tbsp thyme, finely chopped
- 1 tsp salt
- 2 tsp black pepper

Place washed blueberries in a bowl.

Add thyme, salt, and pepper.

Toss together, let sit.

Pastry

- 2½ cups all-purpose flour
- ½ cup plus 1 tsp sugar, divided
- 1 tsp salt
- 1 cup unsalted butter, very cold, cut into ½-inch cubes
- 6 Tbsp ice water
- 1 egg
- ½ cup sugar
- 2 cups vanilla bean ice cream

Add flour, ½ cup sugar, and salt into a food processor. Pulse a few times to mix.

Add about one-fourth of the butter and pulse to gradually incorporate. Continue adding the butter in quarters and pulsing until all of the butter is incorporated, but do not overmix.

Slowly add ice water, pulsing in between.

Dough should be crumbly, but hold together.

Place dough on a clean, dry surface and divide into two balls.

Lightly knead dough until solid but still tender.

Sprinkle with flour, wrap in plastic, and let rest one hour in the refrigerator.

Once removed, let sit until dough reaches room temperature.

Each dough ball will make four pies of each flavor.

Divide each ball into four segments.

Lightly roll each of the four segments out on a floured surface into a 6-inch circles.

For each circle, add 2 tablespoons of pie filling on one-third of the crust.

Gently fold over the empty half, covering the filling.

Use a fork to crimp crusts together, creating mini pies.

Crack the egg into a small bowl and beat lightly until blended. Brush the pies with the egg wash.

Sprinkle sugar over top.

Repeat with second fruit filling.

Bake at 325°F for 10 minutes or until golden brown.

Let cool for 15 minutes.

Serve with one scoop vanilla bean ice cream.

Avocado, Pecan, Cranberry, Black Basmati Pilaf

- 2 cups black basmati rice
- 1 cup pecans, roughly chopped
- 1 cup dried cranberries
- ¼ cup olive oil
- ¼ cup balsamic vinegar
- 2 tsp garlic, finely chopped
- 1 green onion, finely chopped
- 1 Tbsp lemon juice, freshly squeezed
- 1 tsp each salt and pepper
- 1 ripe avocado, scored into cubes and removed from shell

Cook rice with 3 cups of water and a pinch of salt until al dente, approximately 25 minutes.

Drain and let cool in a mixing bowl.

In a mixing bowl, add pecans and cranberries.

In a separate bowl, combine olive oil, vinegar, garlic, green onion, and lemon juice.

Taste and adjust flavor as needed. Season with salt and pepper.

Fold the dressing into pecan mixture.

Add the pecan mixture to the rice.

Using a fork, stir rice so that the dressing covers it.

Pour rice into individual serving bowls, and add fresh avocado on top.

ENDLESS SUMMER

Saturday, July 28th, 2012
Cocktails 7:30pm; Dinner 8:30PM

Thai Watermelon Soup with Fresh Crab, Chili, Lemongrass

Lemon, Honey, Chili Prawns, Sweet Potato Shoestrings

Spicy Tuna Shake, Rattle & Roll
Black Sesame Seared Tuna,
Avocado, Pickled Carrot, Wasabi & Fig Balsamic

Lemongrass & Ginger Beef 'Pops'!
Cucumber, Red Onion, Tomato Salad
Grilled Corn on Cob w/salted herb butter

City S'Mores

Cocktail Included; BYOB for Dinner
Details and Secret Location to be Sent after Seat Reservation

A Life Without Love is Like
a Year without Summer - Swedish Proverb

Endless Summer

Thai Watermelon Soup, Crab, Chili, Lemongrass

Lemon, Honey, and Chili Prawns, Key Lime Vinaigrette,

Sweet Potato Shoestring Fries

Black Sesame Seared Tuna, Avocado, Pickled Carrot, Wasabi, Fig Balsamic

City S'mores

Lemongrass Ginger Beef Pops, Cucumber, Red Onion, and Tomato Salad,

Grilled Corn on the Cob with Wasabi Herb Butter

Serves 4

The Meal

This supper was more casual, more relaxed. It was more of a gathering of friends on a hot summer night who had known each other for years. It was familiar even though everyone was meeting for the first time. The nature of the supper—being outside—had guests kicking off their shoes in preference of the green grass lawn. A self-serve prosecco bar made the event feel like it was at a neighbor's home. Supper was louder than usual with uproars from a joke or an all too familiar story of life in Brooklyn or just life in general. As the sun set, a clip from the movie *The Endless Summer* projected onto the back of the brownstone. In that moment, it really did feel like that—an endless supper. I sat back and just watched everyone having a roaring good time. *This, this is why I do the suppers,* I told myself. I slipped out of my flip-flops, put my feet in the grass, sipped my prosecco, watched the stars up above, and just listened to the laughter.

The Theme

It was the end of July, and Brooklyn was hot, humid, sticky, and mostly abandoned for cooler destinations. What better way to lift the spirits of those that stayed than with a refreshing late-summer supper? The supper was held in a friend's brownstone backyard. I wanted it to feel very casual, like a backyard BBQ. No fancy wine glasses, no fussy floral arrangements. A sommelier friend of mine attended and was pouring cool prosecco and rosé. Guests mingled, sharing stories from the Hamptons and other cooler destinations they frequented. At this point in the summer, it truly felt like an endless summer.

The Setup

One central dining table went down the middle of the grassy backyard. It was covered in a long beach blanket in turquoise tones. White paper bags were filled with some sand and a votive candle burned in each as the sun began to set. Fancy plastic cutlery was set on bright blue trellis-printed cotton napkins and large scallop shells ran down the table holding more small votive candles. Each setting had a clear plastic bag tied with twine and filled with homemade vanilla and chocolate marshmallows, a graham cracker, and a piece of prettily wrapped milk chocolate. S'mores were the takeaway gift!

Thai Watermelon Soup, Crab, Chili, Lemongrass

- 1 medium seedless watermelon
- 2 Tbsp olive oil, divided
- ½ cup white onion, finely chopped
- 3 Tbsp garlic, finely chopped
- 1 Tbsp fresh lemongrass, finely chopped
- 1 Thai chili, finely chopped
- ½ cup fresh basil, finely chopped
- 1 tsp ginger, grated
- Juice of 2 limes
- 1 tsp salt
- 1 tsp pepper
- 2 cups crabmeat
- 1 Tbsp olive oil
- 1 Tbsp fine chopped garlic
- ½ cup Italian parsley, finely chopped
- 1 Tbsp white wine (pinot grigio)
- 1 avocado
- 2 Tbsp crème fraîche

Using a melon baller, scoop watermelon into a large mixing bowl.

Add 1 tablespoon olive oil, onion, garlic, lemongrass, chili, basil, and ginger to a sauté pan.

Over medium heat, cook for 4–5 minutes until softened.

Remove from heat, add lime juice.

In a blender, puree watermelon and contents of the sauté pan.

(Best to puree in small batches given the volume of watermelon.)

Add salt and pepper to taste.

Chill in refrigerator at least one hour, or overnight for stronger flavor.

Just before serving, in a sauté pan, add crab meat with 1 tablespoon olive oil, garlic, parsley, and white wine.

Season with salt and pepper.

Sauté for 4–5 minutes until crab is just browning.

Slice avocado into 1-inch slivers.

In chilled soup bowls or martini glasses, add 2 tablespoons crab meat.

Ladle 2 cups chilled watermelon mixture over crab meat.

Garnish with 2 avocado slices.

Grind a small bit of black pepper over top.

Dollop 1 teaspoon crème fraîche over center of bowl or serving glass.

Serve chilled.

Lemon, Honey, and Chili Grilled Prawns,
Key Lime Vinaigrette,
Sweet Potato Shoestring Fries

Lemon, Honey, and Chili Grilled Prawns with Key Lime Vinaigrette

- Juice from 1 lemon

- 1 Tbsp honey

- 3 Tbsp olive oil, divided

- 4 cloves garlic, finely chopped, divided

- 1 Tbsp chili powder

- 4 wooden skewers, pre-soaked in water to prevent burning on grill

In a mixing bowl, add lemon juice, honey, 2 tablespoons olive oil, 3 cloves chopped garlic, and chili powder.

Whisk until blended.

Add cleaned prawns to the bowl. Toss and let marinate for 20 minutes.

Skewer shrimp (4 or 5 prawns on each skewer).

In another mixing bowl, add lime juice, 1 tablespoon olive oil, vinegar, chili flakes, Dijon, and 1 clove finely chopped garlic.

Whisk until blended. Set aside.

Grill prawns over medium heat for 6 minutes (3 minutes each side).

- 16–20 prawns, cleaned
  and deveined

- Juice from 2 key lime

- 2 Tbsp white wine vinegar

- 1 Tbsp red chili flakes

- 1 tsp Dijon mustard

Brush marinade over prawns once every minute of cooking to keep tender.

Remove from grill and place on a cookie sheet.

Pour key lime vinaigrette over prawn skewers.

Sweet Potato Shoestring Fries

- 2 sweet potatoes, peeled
  and julienned

- 2 cups olive oil

- 2 tsp salt

- 2 Tbsp chili powder, divided

Rinse julienned potatoes under cold water to remove any excess starch.

Dry them thoroughly with a towel or salad spinner. They must be very dry to fry.

Bring 3 inches of olive oil to 360°F in a heavy-bottomed, deep pot.

Fry potatoes for 4 minutes, in small batches, being sure not to overcrowd the pot.

Remove fries with a slotted spoon and place onto a clean, dry paper towel.

Immediately season with salt and chili powder, while still hot.

Serve one prawn skewer per person with a small handful of potato fries on an appetizer plate.

Black Sesame Seared Tuna, Avocado, Pickled Carrot, Wasabi, Fig Balsamic

- 2 cups sushi rice
- 2 lb ahi tuna steaks
- 1 cup black sesame seeds
- 1 cup balsamic vinegar
- 1 tsp sugar
- 1 tsp black pepper
- 2 fresh figs, diced
- Saran wrap
- 1 avocado, diced
- 1 carrot, pickled and diced
- 2 tsp fresh wasabi

Per packaging instructions, cook rice. Set aside to cool.

Cut tuna into 8 equal cubes.

Slice cubes three quarters of the way through and set aside.

Place sesame seeds on a plate and set aside.

In a small saucepan over low heat, combine balsamic vinegar, sugar, black pepper, and figs.

Stir until combined and reduced into a light syrup.

It's ready when sauce sticks to a spoon, about 5 minutes.

Cover a work area with saran wrap cut into 2 x 4-inch rectangles.

Individually lay open the tuna pieces and layer with two pieces each of avocado and carrot.

Close tuna rectangles.

Cover tuna rectangles with ¼ cup of sushi rice.

Roll rice around tuna, making sure all sides are covered.

Roll tuna and rice rectangles across black sesame seeds, ensuring even coverage.

Plate 2 rolls per plate and drizzle with 1 tsp balsamic fig reduction.

Garnish with a ½ tsp fresh wasabi.

Serve.

City S'mores

- 8 graham crackers, halved
- 8 chocolate squares, milk or dark chocolate

This one is a bit of a cheat, as I prefer to buy the mini graham crackers and the chocolate squares.

I bought some clear cellophane bags and blue grosgrain ribbon.

- 4 cellophane bags

- 4 ribbons of grosgrain ribbon

Homemade Marshmallows

- 1 sheet parchment paper large enough to cover a baking dish

- 3 cups sugar

- 1 cup light corn syrup

- ¼ tsp salt

- 2 cups water, divided

- 4 packages gelatin, unflavored

- 2 tsp pure vanilla extract

- 1 tsp powdered chocolate

- 1 tsp powdered strawberry

- Vegetable oil for brushing

- 1 ½ cups confectioners' sugar

In each bag I placed 1 wooden skewer, 4 mini graham crackers, 2 chocolate squares, and 2 homemade marshmallows: 1 strawberry and 1 chocolate.

I put the bags on each guest's folded napkin.

After dinner, we gathered around the outdoor fire, cooked the s'mores and watched *The Endless Summer* projected onto a flat bed sheet hung in the yard where we had supper.

Lightly oil a baking dish.

Line it with parchment paper and oil the paper.

In a medium saucepan, add sugar, corn syrup, salt, and 1 ¼ cups water.

Bring to a boil over high heat, stirring constantly to dissolve sugar.

Once dissolved, continue to cook (no stirring) another 7 minutes.

Remove from heat.

Add remaining water and gelatin to a mixing bowl. Let sit 5 minutes to soften gelatin.

Divide the mixture into 2 parts.

Using an electric hand mixer, slowly combine half of the warm sugar mixture to half of the gelatin.

Increase speed gradually and beat until stiff.

Beat in vanilla and either the chocolate or strawberry powder.

Pour into a casserole or baking dish and make smooth with a spatula.

Let rest, uncovered, for 3 hours or until firm.

Repeat with remaining warm sugar mixture to make other flavor.

Sift 1 ½ cups confectioners' sugar onto a work surface.

Unmold marshmallows onto the sugared surface, removing parchment.

Oil a sharp knife and cut marshmallows into 3-inch squares or to your liking.

Roll each square in the sifted ½ cup of confectioners' sugar.

Shake off excess sugar.

Place two marshmallows in each of the cellophane bags with the graham crackers and chocolate.

Lemongrass Ginger Beef Pops, Cucumber, Red Onion, and Tomato Salad, Grilled Corn on the Cob with Wasabi Herb Butter

Lemongrass Ginger Beef Pops

- 1 lb beef filet, cut into 3-inch cubes
- 1 Tbsp lemongrass, finely chopped
- 1 Tbsp ginger puree
- Salt and pepper
- 4 bamboo skewers, soaked in water

In a mixing bowl, add beef cubes, lemongrass, and ginger. Season lightly with salt and pepper. Toss the beef to coat.

Add 3–4 pieces beef on each skewer, stacked on top of each other at one end of the stick with no space between them.

Grill over medium heat for 10 minutes or to 140°F on a meat thermometer.

Serve as a passed appetizer with a cocktail napkin.

Cucumber, Red Onion, and Tomato Salad

- 1 English cucumber, roughly chopped
- 1 small red onion, peeled and finely chopped
- 4 heirloom tomatoes, roughly chopped
- 1 Tbsp red wine vinaigrette
- 1 Tbsp olive oil
- 1 tsp sea salt
- 1 tsp fresh ground black pepper

Add all ingredients in a mixing bowl and stir to combine.

Taste for seasoning and adjust if needed.

Grilled Corn on the Cob with Wasabi Herb Butter

- 4 ears white corn

- 1 stick unsalted butter

- 2 tsp wasabi paste

- Salt and pepper, to taste

Remove top layer of husk from each ear of corn to prevent them from catching fire over the grill.

Grill corn in their husks for 20 minutes over medium heat. Basically, the corn is steaming inside the husks.

Remove the corn from grill. Remove husks using gloves so as not to burn your fingers.

Melt butter in a small bowl. Add a pinch of salt and pepper to the melted butter. Mix in wasabi paste and stir to combine.

Brush each ear of corn with wasabi butter.

Serve.

Food & Farms, A Spring Supper

Roasted Asparagus, Radish, Marinated Feta

Trout Cake, Dill Red Bliss Potatoes, Horseradish Crème Fraîche

Mint, Apple, Rack of Lamb, Couscous, Fennel, Pine Nut, Rocket

Lemon and Rosemary Tart, Hibiscus Sauce, Blueberry

Serves 4

The Meal

Having a wine partner on this supper versus the usual BYOB created a different vibe around the tables. As the courses were presented, the sommelier also spoke to the wine pairings. It felt a bit fancier, a bit more choreographed. By the third course and pairing, the fancy had fallen to fun! Guests had been tucked away on their farms and homes over the winter. The tables were full of discussions of how the long winter was spent and where they were now in planting their new spring/summer gardens. It was lively, it was refreshing! By the fifth pairing, the conversation turned much livelier with talks of all the gossip missed through the winter. Once again, guests lingered long after the dessert course. This time, I quietly slipped back to the farmhouse front porch and settled into a rocking chair. Hearing the outbreak of laughter, the sudden whispers, and the sharing of stories as nature went to bed was the perfect ending to the supper.

The Theme

By popular demand, I was asked back to do another supper in Georgia. Posh Picnic had been a great success, and the locals that didn't come to the first supper had requested an encore. I love being on the farm in the spring, so it was an easy decision to make. The theme had to be about the awakening of spring in the mountains and on the farm. The baby chicks had hatched, new puppies had been born, the birds were singing their messages of spring's arrival, and the air was finally warm enough after the winter to eat outdoors again under the open-air tent. The menu was completely inspired by what was hatching and harvesting on the local farms. Baby asparagus, fennel, rocket, and radishes picked fresh from the garden. Local spring trout caught early that morning. A local winemaker attended this supper and offered a wine pairing for each course. It was a delicious celebration of spring.

The Setup

The long tables were dressed in mint green linens and colorful cotton napkins printed in a whimsical pattern in pastel colors. Instead of floral arrangements, I put small arrangements of herbs from the garden inside bright pink satin bags tied with gold ribbon and attached to a collage I created of all things spring! Small, clear glass votives with simple white candles would soon illuminate the table after sunset. A pile of light shawls and thin blankets were stacked on a bench in case the air became too cool after dusk. Natural-colored wedding chairs down the table brought the table setting back to nature.

The Brooklyn Suppers

Roasted Asparagus, Radish, Marinated Feta

- 1 lb block feta cheese

- 2 cups olive oil, divided

- 1 Tbsp fresh thyme, finely chopped

- 1 Tbsp fresh rosemary, finely chopped

- 1 Tbsp oregano, finely chopped

- 2 cloves garlic

- 1 tsp black peppercorns

- Juice from 1 lemon

- 1 tsp red pepper flakes

- 1 lb green asparagus, ends cut, rinsed and dried

- 1 lb red/pink radishes, tops and ends cut, rinsed, dried, and cut into 1/4-inch slices, widthwise

- 1 Tbsp white balsamic vinegar

- 2 tsp salt and pepper for final plating of the dishes

In a plastic bowl with lid or in a plastic resealable bag, add feta, 1 cup olive oil, chopped herbs, garlic cloves, peppercorns, lemon juice, and red pepper flakes.

Be sure the block is completely submerged.

Seal the container and leave at room temperature for 4 hours to marinate.

Meanwhile, place prepped asparagus on a baking tray.

Add 1/2 cup olive oil and season with salt and pepper.

Toss so oil completely coats the spears.

Roast in a preheated 350°F oven for 25 minutes.

Spears should be al dente.

Treat sliced radishes the same way, but add 1 tablespoon white balsamic vinegar along with the 1/2 cup olive oil. Roast along with the asparagus.

Remove feta from marinade and cut into four slices.

On your appetizer plates, layer 4—6 slices of radish, then one slice of feta, then 3–4 asparagus stems on top.

Season lightly with salt and pepper.

Serve.

Trout Cake, Dill Red Bliss Potatoes, Horseradish Crème Fraîche

Trout Cakes

- 2 cups smoked trout

- 2 tsp green onion, finely chopped

- 2 tsp capers, drained

- ½ tsp grated lemon peel

- 1 tsp black pepper, ground

- Salt, to taste

- 1 egg, beaten

- ¼ cup whipping cream

- 1 cup breadcrumbs, divided

- 2 Tbsp olive oil

- 2 Tbsp chives, finely chopped

In a mixing bowl, combine trout, green onion, capers, and lemon peel.

Add black pepper and season with salt.

Add egg, cream, and ½ cup of breadcrumbs.

Blend together.

Form ½-cup trout cakes, making four ½-inch cakes.

Pour remaining ½ cup breadcrumbs onto a plate.

Roll fish cakes in breadcrumbs for a light coating.

Add 2 tablespoons olive oil to a sauté pan and bring to medium heat.

Sauté cakes on both sides until golden brown, approximately 6 minutes per side.

Serve with a small dollop of horseradish crème fraîche on top and a sprinkle of chives.

Horseradish Crème Fraîche

- 1 cup crème fraîche
- 2 Tbsp fresh horseradish
- 1 garlic clove, minced
- 1 tsp lemon juice, freshly squeezed
- ½ tsp cayenne pepper
- ½ tsp black pepper, ground
- Salt, to taste

Combine all ingredients in a small mixing bowl.

Season to taste with salt.

Cover and keep refrigerated until ready to serve with trout cakes.

Dill Red Bliss Potatoes

- 8–10 red bliss potatoes, washed and cut into 2-inch cubes
- 1 Tbsp salt
- 1 Tbsp olive oil
- 1 Tbsp butter
- ½ cup fresh dill, finely chopped
- 2 tsp jalapeño, finely chopped
- Salt and pepper, to taste

Add potatoes to a pot of boiling, lightly salted water.

Cook 12 minutes or until easily sliced with a knife.

Drain potatoes and place in a mixing bowl.

Add olive oil, butter, dill, and jalapeno. Stir to combine.

Season as needed with salt and pepper.

Mint, Apple, Rack of Lamb
Couscous, Fennel, Pine Nut, Rocket

Mint, Apple, Rack of Lamb

- 1 frenched lamb rib rack with 8–10 ribs

- ½ cup fresh mint, finely chopped

- 2 cloves garlic, finely chopped

- 2 Tbsp olive oil

- Salt and pepper

- 2 Gala apples, finely chopped

- ½ cup white wine

- ½ cup vegetable stock

Using a large resealable bag, add lamb, mint, garlic, olive oil, and a pinch each of salt and pepper.

Toss together on all sides, ensuring lamb is well coated.

Let marinate overnight in the refrigerator or at least for a few hours.

Let it come to room temperature before cooking.

Preheat oven to 450°F.

Wrap exposed bones in foil.

Score fat one inch apart, then dash with salt and pepper.

Place lamb and marinade on a sheet pan, fat side up.

Roast at 450°F for 10 minutes, then lower to 300°F for another 10–15 minutes until a meat thermometer reads 135°F for medium rare.

When resting, lamb temperature will rise to 140°F.

If a more well-done lamb is preferred, cook to 145°F.

Let rest 20 minutes.

In the meantime, make the apple pan sauce.

Add apples to a sauce pan. Add white wine, let simmer, and reduce until all liquid has been absorbed.

Add stock and reduce again until liquid is absorbed.

To serve, cut lamb chops away from rack, slicing between the bones.

Place chops on a serving platter, overlapping the bones to form a ring or circle.

Pour pan sauce over meat.

Couscous, Fennel, Pine Nut, Rocket

- 1 fennel bulb, washed, bottom and stems cut off
- 1 Tbsp olive oil
- 2 tsp each salt and pepper, divided
- ½ cup pine nuts, toasted
- 1 lb rocket greens (arugula), rinsed
- 2 cups couscous
- 1 cup vegetable stock
- 1 cup water
- ½ cup currant

Brush fennel bulb with olive oil and lightly season with 1 teaspoon each of salt and pepper.

Roast in a 350°F oven for 40 minutes.

Remove, let cool, then finely chop.

In a dry, lightly salted sauté pan, add pine nuts.

Over medium heat, brown nuts.

Remove and let cool.

Roughly chop rocket greens.

Pour dry couscous into a mixing bowl.

Pour vegetable stock and water into a saucepan.

Bring to a boil.

Remove from heat and slowly pour over couscous until fully absorbed.

Cover with a tea towel and set aside for 15 minutes.

Remove towel and lightly fluff couscous with a fork. I like to just lightly rake a fork across the top, back and forth, until all of the couscous has been through the fork. It should be light and airy.

Add fennel, rocket greens, and currants to the couscous and toss to combine.

Season with the remaining salt and pepper, to taste.

Serve with lamb chops.

Lemon and Rosemary Tart, Hibiscus Sauce, Blueberry

- 1 cup pine nuts

- 1 cup sugar, divided

- 3 cups flour

- 2 tsp fresh rosemary, finely chopped

- 8 oz unsalted butter, room temperature

- 3 large eggs, plus 2 egg yolks, divided

- 1 tsp vanilla extract

- ½ cup lemon juice, freshly squeezed

- 6 Tbsp unsalted butter, cold

- 1 cup fresh blueberries

Using a mixer, chop pine nuts, add ¼ cup sugar, flour, and rosemary.

Mix well.

Set aside.

In a separate mixing bowl, add butter, 1 egg, and vanilla.

Mix until combined.

Add dry ingredients to the wet ingredients.

Mix until combined.

Wrap dough in plastic wrap and refrigerate for 10 minutes.

Divide dough into four parts and freeze 3 for future tarts.

Preheat oven to 375°F.

Lightly butter a tart pan (either a single large tart, 4 medium tarts, or 12 bite-size tarts).

Line each tart pan with dough and use fingers to spread evenly across bottom and up the sides.

Prick dough lightly with a fork.

Bake for 10 minutes.

Press down any air bubbles and rotate pan.

Bake another 10 minutes.

Remove and let cool.

Set up a double boiler, andbring water to a boil. If you do not have a double broiler, a mixing bowl over a small pot filled with ½ cup water works fine.

In the mixing bowl, add 2 large eggs, 2 large egg yolks, and ¾ cup sugar.

Whisk ingredients together.

Whisk over heat continuously and evenly in the bowl for 2 minutes.

Eggs should be foamy and beginning to thicken.

Add ⅓ of the lemon juice.

Whisk continually until it thickens again.

Repeat, adding ⅓ of lemon juice twice more until the ½ cup of lemon juice has been added.

Whisk lemon filling until thick and light in color.

Turn off heat and add 6 tablespoons cold butter, 1 tablespoon at a time.

Filling will thicken as it cools.

Spoon filling into tart shell(s).

Add a single fresh blueberry in the center of each individual tart or 3 to 5 across a large tart.

Hibiscus Sauce

- 3 cups hibiscus juice
- 1 cup sugar
- 1 tsp vanilla extract

Add all ingredients in a saucepan and cook over medium heat.

Stir often until juice cooks down into a syrup.

Remove from heat. Let cool.

Serve individual large tarts on a dessert plate with 1 tablespoon of the hibiscus sauce on the bottom of the plate.

Serve bite-sized tarts on a serving platter with a drop of the hibiscus sauce directly in the center of each tart.

"When spring came, there were no problems except where to be happiest."—Ernest Hemingway, *A Movable Feast*

Midsummer Farm Bakes, Brews, and Bonfires

Summer Succotash

Watermelon, Feta, Mint

Shrimp, Clam, Andouille Bake, Hush Puppies

Seared Scallops, Chilled Apple, Celery, Lemon, Basil

Sweet Cornbread, Strawberry Peach Shortcakes

Serves 4

The Meal

Guests arrived from the hot, humid Brooklyn outdoors into a cool, breezy, beachy, brownstone environment. My little window unit on the fourth floor was working hard to keep it cool inside. Guests arrived with their favorite specialty craft beers or summer white wines, both the perfect drink for a bake. Uniquely, this supper found guests lingering, chatting, and hanging out versus sitting down to the table. As the courses were served, they sat for a few minutes but found it more comfortable to be standing and socializing. So, we gathered around the table as food came and went. It was fun and energetic. It was so lively that I may have gotten a knock at my door from my neighbor below. The Clambake Supper Club in Brooklyn was so successful I decided to repeat it in Georgia as I was due to put on another supper there later in the month. I used the same table setting style with the brown parchment paper covered tables under the outdoor tent. When a supper was that successful, might as well do it twice!

The Theme

Growing up in the South, there were always clambakes at the beach over the summer. A clambake, a bonfire, and usually a few craft beers or crisp white wines were the required elements. It turns out that New Yorkers have a thing for them too. I decided to host a supper based around a traditional clambake, but with a few twists. The table would look and feel like an outdoor bake, but would actually be in my brownstone apartment.

The Setup

The table was covered in brown paper with big cutlery drawings on it. I found the roll at a local paper store, and knew I could do so many things with it for my suppers. I sprinkled sand across the table imitating the beach and used mason jars and white paper bags to hold white votive candles. Cotton napkins in an Indian block-print design with shades of blue were placed under the menus. A few tall, grassy stalks were on the ends of the table representing the tall reeds found near the beach.

Mid-Summer Farm Bakes, Brews & Bonfires

Summer Succotash
House Made Pizza

Watermelon, Feta, Mint

Seared, Chilled Scallop,
(Apple, Celery, Lemon, Basil)

Shrimp, Clam, Andoille Bake
Hush Puppies

Sweet Cornbread Strawberry
& Peach Shortcakes

featuring; Martyn House Home Brews
& Paired Wines w/each course

*Love is to the heart
what the summer is to the farmer's year -
it brings to harvest all the loveliest flowers
of the soul. ~Author Unknown*

Summer Succotash

- 2 cups fresh lima beans
- 1 cup red onion, finely chopped
- 1 cup fresh okra, sliced into ½-inch slices
- 1 tsp garlic, finely chopped
- 3 cups fresh corn kernels
- 1 tsp salt
- 1 tsp black pepper
- 3 Tbsp butter
- 1 cup cherry tomatoes, halved
- ½ cup fresh basil (chiffonade)
- 1 baguette, cut into ½-inch slices on the diagonal

In a medium saucepan, add 2 cups of water and lima beans.

Bring to a boil over medium heat, reduce to low.

Simmer beans until tender, approximately 10 minutes.

Drain and set aside.

In a sauté pan, add the onion, okra, and garlic.

Cook over medium heat until tender, about 6 minutes.

Add corn kernels, salt, pepper, and drained beans.

Cook altogether until tender, approximately 6 minutes.

Add butter and stir until all ingredients are coated.

Remove from heat.

Add cherry tomatoes and basil.

Toss together and serve in small tasting bowls or on toasted baguette slices, bruschetta style.

Watermelon, Feta, Mint

- 1 cup fresh mint, finely chopped, reserve 4 mint leaves for garnish
- 1 cup olive oil
- 1 cup balsamic vinegar
- Salt and pepper, to taste
- 1 small watermelon, cut into 1-inch cubes
- Feta cheese, cut into 1 x 3-inch slices

In a small mixing bowl, combine chopped mint, olive oil, vinegar, and salt and pepper.

Whisk together until well combined.

On individual appetizer plates or one large serving platter, layer four watermelon cubes, creating a square.

Next layer 1 feta slice over the watermelon cubes.

Pour 1 tablespoon of dressing over the feta.

Garnish with a mint leaf.

Serve.

Shrimp, Clam, Andouille Bake, Hush Puppies

- 1 bottle dry white wine

- 10 cups water

- 2 Tbsp Old Bay seasoning, divided

- 1 tsp red chili flakes

- 4 cloves garlic, whole

- 1 bunch of fresh thyme, tied with string

- 2 lb small new potatoes, whole

In a 30-quart pot, add wine and water.

Place a steamer basket in the pot.

Bring to a boil, then add 1 tablespoon Old Bay seasoning, chili flakes, garlic, and thyme bunch.

Add potatoes and cook for 5 minutes.

Add corn and sausages and cook 5 more minutes.

Add shrimp and cook 5 minutes.

Add clams and cook until they open.

The Brooklyn Suppers

- 4 ears yellow corn, husked and halved
- 4 links andouille sausages, cut into 2-inch pieces
- 16–20 medium shrimp, peeled and deveined
- 12–15 steamer soft shell clams, scrubbed
- 1 stick salted butter
- 2 lemons, quartered

Remove pot from heat.

Using a slotted spoon, remove contents onto a large serving platter or onto a newspaper covered table.

Sprinkle remaining Old Bay seasoning over the bake.

Melt butter and serve in small ramekins or paper cups with serving bowls with quartered lemons on the side.

Strain and pour broth into a pitcher and serve on the table.

Hush Puppies

- Vegetable oil for frying
- 1½ cups cornmeal
- 2 Tbsp all-purpose flour
- 3 tsp baking powder
- 4 tsp sugar
- 2 tsp salt
- ¼ tsp red chili flakes
- ½ cup sweet onion, finely chopped
- 2 large eggs, beaten
- ¾ cup light beer

In a heavy-bottom pan, add 2 inches of oil.

Heat oil to 350°F.

In a mixing bowl, add cornmeal, flour, baking powder, sugar, salt, and chili flakes.

Stir to combine well.

Add onion and eggs.

Add beer.

Stir to combine into a smooth batter.

In batches, drop rounded tablespoons of batter into the oil.

Fry for 3 minutes until golden brown, turning often.

*An ice cream scoop works well for consistent-sized puppies.

Remove from pan with a slotted spoon and transfer onto a paper towel-covered cooling rack to cool and drain excess oil.

Serve in 2–3 bowls across the table.

Seared Scallops, Chilled Apple, Celery, Lemon, Basil

- ½ cup olive oil

- 12 sea scallops, rinsed and patted dry

- 1 Granny Smith apple, peeled, cored, and cut into ½-inch pieces

- 2 stalks celery, rinsed and cut horizontally into ¼-inch slices

- Juice of 1 lemon

- Salt and pepper

- ½ cup fresh basil (chiffonade)

Add olive oil to a sauté pan over medium-high heat.

When it begins to sizzle, add scallops, flat sides down.

Brown on bottom for 2 minutes, then flip over to brown the other side for another 2 minutes.

Remove from pan and set onto a paper towel.

In same sauté pan, add apple, celery, and lemon juice.

Add salt and pepper.

Sauté, stirring often until apples are soft.

Remove from heat.

Plate two scallops on an appetizer plate.

Spoon 1–2 tsp of apple mixture over scallops.

Garnish lightly with basil.

This dish could be scaled into an entrée portion by adding jasmine rice and 4 scallops per plate.

The Brooklyn Suppers

Sweet Cornbread, Strawberry Peach Shortcakes

- 1 cup all-purpose flour
- 1 cup yellow cornmeal
- ⅔ cup plus 2 tsp white sugar, divided
- 1 tsp salt
- 3½ tsp baking powder
- 1 egg
- 1 cup whole milk
- ⅓ cup vegetable oil
- 2 cups strawberries, washed and cut into quarters
- 2 cups white peaches, washed and cut into quarters
- 2 cups whipping cream
- 2 tsp granulated white sugar
- ½ tsp vanilla extract

Preheat oven to 400°F.

Lightly grease a 9-inch cake pan.

In a mixing bowl combine flour, cornmeal, sugar, salt, and baking powder.

Stir in egg, milk, and oil.

Combine well.

Pour batter into cake pan and cook for 25 minutes. When done, a toothpick should come out clean from the center.

Let cool, then cut into 3-inch squares.

Remove squares from pan and slice in half horizontally so there is a top and bottom.

In a mixing bowl, combine strawberries and peaches, plus 1 teaspoon sugar.

Set aside.

In another bowl, add whipping cream, 1 teaspoon sugar, and vanilla.

Either hand beat with a whisk or use a mixer to whip the cream until soft peaks form.

On dessert plates, place the bottom half of the cornbread squares.

Top with a hearty spoonful of fruit.

Place the top of the cornbread on the fruit at an angle so the fruit is not entirely covered.

Dollop a tablespoon of fresh whipped cream on top of the cornbread.

Serve.

Falling Into Autumn
Saturday, September 28th, 2013

Grilled Eggplant, Taleggio, Hen of Wood, Pomegranates
Butternut Squash Soup, Pumpernickel Crouton, Lardons
Cider Risotto, Pancetta, Parmesan, Fried Sage
GA Quail, Fig, Vidalias, Swede & Sweet Potatoe Mash
Apple Crumble, Sharp White Cheddar

Beer &/or Wine Pairing Included
$75
Chef, Heather Antonelli (Author of Haute n the Kitchen)
Reserve Seats at www.themartynhouse.com

Falling into Autumn

Grilled Eggplant, Taleggio, Hen of the Wood Mushroom, Pomegranates

Apple Crumble, Sharp White Cheddar

Cider Risotto, Pancetta, Parmigiano-Reggiano, Fried Sage

Quail, Fig, Vidalia Mash

Butternut Squash Soup, Pumpernickel Croutons, Lardons

The Meal

This started out as the quietest supper I had hosted so far. It was as if everyone knew winter was just around the corner and the harvest season was coming to a close. Conversations were intimate and almost whispered across the tables. As soon as supper was finished, the guests took one of the stacked blankets and headed to the big bonfire. All it takes is a good fire to stir the mood apparently. Suddenly everyone was exchanging stories of places and memories over the past year. Stories that kept them there well into the night.

The Theme

As much as I love autumn in New York, it's also pretty spectacular in the South. I was headed down to visit my family for a long weekend on the Georgia farm when I got a call from my mom. Since you are going to be here…how about hosting a supper?

During the long drive down from Brooklyn to Georgia, I came up with a seasonal menu and theme. Falling into Autumn was all about those cozy flavors and dishes we start to think about as summer fades to fall. Rich creamy risottos, butternut squash soup, and apple pie are the flavors most craved in autumn for me. Five rather decadent courses to feed your stomach and your soul. There would be a big bonfire after the meal with warm blankets and hot toddies.

The Setup

The event tent on the farm had changed into a beautiful, warm, rich orange color. It was the perfect surrounding for an autumn theme, a theme that could be easily created in any home. The long tables were scattered with pinecones and leaves gathered from the farm floor. Cut-out pumpkin- and leaf-shaped papers held the guests' names and wonderful quotes about the season from famous writers and poets. The cotton block-printed napkins were orange and purple with a pretty vine pattern. It was the fall floor brought onto the table.

Grilled Eggplant, Taleggio, Hen of the Wood Mushroom, Pomegranates

- 1 large American eggplant

- ¼ tsp cayenne pepper

- ¼ tsp curry powder

- ¼ tsp coriander powder

- ¼ tsp onion powder

- ½ cup olive oil

- 4 hen of the woods mushrooms (each piece being at least 3 stems)

- ½ cup soy sauce

- 1 lb Taleggio cheese

- 1 cup pomegranate seeds, rinsed

Slice eggplant crosswise into 1-inch thick slices.

In a small mixing bowl, combine cayenne, curry, coriander, and onion powders.

Rub both sides of each eggplant slice with olive oil to coat.

Heat either a grill or grill pan to medium.

Grill eggplant 3 minutes each side or until softened, but retaining shape.

Remove from heat.

Brush hen of the woods with soy sauce to lightly coat, not marinate.

Grill mushrooms 3 minutes, turn and grill 3 more minutes until softened but not wilted.

Slice the cheese into ½-inch slices lengthwise, ending with approximate 3 x 2-inch slices.

Place eggplant on either single appetizer plates or a serving platter.

Top next with Taleggio, then mushrooms. Lastly, sprinkle pomegranate seeds over top.

Serve.

Apple Crumble, Sharp White Cheddar

- 2 lb Granny Smith apples, peeled, cored, and cut into 3/5-inch cubes
- 1 cup plus 1 Tbsp white flour, divided
- ½ cup white sugar
- 2 Tbsp lemon juice
- 1½ tsp ground cinnamon, divided
- 1 cup rolled oats
- 1 cup brown sugar
- ½ tsp baking powder
- ½ cup unsalted butter, melted
- ½ tsp salt
- 4 ½ slices white cheddar cheese

Preheat oven to 350°F.

In a mixing bowl, add apples, 1 tablespoon flour, sugar, lemon juice, and ½ tsp cinnamon.

Toss together then spread evenly in a 1½-quart baking dish.

In a mixing bowl, combine oats, 1 cup flour, brown sugar, baking powder, 1 teaspoon cinnamon, butter, and salt.

Mix until small clumps form.

Spread over apples, crumbling with fingers as you spread it out.

Bake 35 minutes until golden brown.

Remove from oven and let cool for 10 minutes.

Serve on small plates or bowls with cheese slices leaning against the crumble.

Cider Risotto, Pancetta, Parmigiano-Reggiano, Fried Sage

- ¼ cup plus 2 tsp olive oil, divided
- 2 cups arborio rice
- 4 cups chicken stock, divided
- 4 cups apple cider, fresh, divided
- 1 tsp salt
- 3 tsp black pepper, divided
- 2 cups Parmigiano-Reggiano cheese, grated finely
- ½ lb pancetta, thin slices from butcher
- 8 sage leaves, fried in olive oil and drained on paper towels

In a deep sauté pan, warm ¼ cup olive oil over medium heat.

Add rice and stir constantly until rice has absorbed olive oil and is glistening but not toasted.

Add 1 cup chicken stock so that it covers the rice.

Wait 3 minutes, then begin stirring until stock is absorbed.

Add 1 cup apple cider and stir constantly until rice has absorbed the cider.

Repeat, alternating stock and cider until risotto has tripled in size and is al dente using all 8 cups of liquid together.

Be sure it does not overcook or become mushy.

Add 1 teaspoon each of salt and pepper.

Stir in cheese and mix to incorporate.

In a frying pan, add pancetta slices and individually fry in 1 teaspoon of olive oil until crunchy like bacon.

In same frying pan with 1 teaspoon olive oil, fry sage leaves, turning once while frying.

Leaves should be crunchy in texture.

Place pancetta and sage on a paper towel to absorb excess oil.

In serving bowls, add 1 cup risotto.

Top with crunchy pancetta slices and two fried sage leaves.

Grind 2 teaspoons fresh black pepper over risotto.

Quail, Fig, Vidalia Mash

Quail

- 4 semi-boneless quail, rinsed and patted dry
- ½ cup olive oil
- 8 fresh figs, cut into quarters
- 1 Vidalia onion, finely chopped
- ½ cup balsamic vinegar
- 1 tsp Dijon mustard
- 1 tsp fresh thyme, finely chopped
- ½ cup red wine

Sear quail over medium heat, turning once, in a sauté pan with ½ cup olive oil until browned.

Add figs to pan and let soften.

Whisk together onion, vinegar, Dijon, thyme, and red wine.

Pour over quail in sauté pan.

Stir to combine sauce and coat quail.

Remove quail once coated and transfer to a clean plate.

Add red wine to pan and cook with pan juices until reduced into a rich sauce.

Set aside to pour over quail once plated.

Mash

- 1 swede, peeled and chopped into medium-sized chunks
- 1 sweet potato, peeled and chopped into medium-sized chunks
- 2 carrots, peeled and chopped into medium-sized chunks
- 2 parsnips, peeled and chopped into medium-sized chunks
- 1 stick salted butter
- 1 cup crème fraîche
- ½ cup heavy cream

Fill a deep pot with swede, potato, carrot, and parsnip chunks.

Add water to cover vegetables.

Cook over medium heat until vegetables are tender, not mushy.

Drain vegetables into a strainer over the sink.

Put vegetables back into pot and add butter and crème fraîche.

Using a hand held masher, combine root vegetables with butter and crème fraiche until creamy and smooth.

Add heavy cream and stir to combine until the consistency is smooth and silky.

To plate, ladle one heaping scoop of mash onto dinner plates.

Place quail against mash.

Spoon pan juices over both.

Serve.

Butternut Squash Soup, Pumpernickel Croutons, Lardons

- 1 butternut squash, halved

- 1 cup olive oil

- 1 tsp nutmeg

- 1 tsp honey

- 8–10 cups vegetable broth

- 2 tsp black pepper, divided

- 2 tsp salt, divided

- 1 loaf pumpernickel bread, sliced into 1-inch square cubes

- ½ lb slab bacon, cut into ¼-inch cubes

Brush both halves of butternut squash with olive oil, nutmeg, and honey.

Roast in oven at 350°F for 45 minutes.

Remove from oven, let cool, then scoop out the squash and put into a stock pot.

Add vegetable broth.

Cook over low heat for 15 minutes, stirring often.

Turn off burner.

Using a hand blender, puree soup until creamy.

Add 1 teaspoon each salt and pepper.

Cover to keep warm.

Put cubed pumpernickel squares on a sheet pan and toss lightly with olive oil and 1 teaspoon each salt and pepper.

Bake in the oven at 350°F until toasted on the outside but still somewhat soft on the inside.

In a sauté pan, add slab bacon cubes and sauté over medium heat until firm with a hard exterior but soft interior. It's not bacon bits—its lardons!

Warm soup bowls in the oven.

Pour 2 cups soup into bowls.

Garnish with 1 or 2 croutons and a sprinkle of lardons.

Serve.

September's Serenade

Olive, Sun-kissed Tomato Cornbread Biscuits

Pan-Seared Trout with Lemon Jus, Peppered Couscous, Roasted Fennel

Rosemary Pork Tenderloin, Wilted Greens, Balsamic Beets, Mustard Stout Beer Sauce

Apple Pear Cinnamon Cake, Salted Caramel Sauce

The Meal

Once everyone settled into their seats and had drinks in hand, I gave my usual greeting and thanks for coming. Before bringing out the first course, I told the guests that the pencils and paper were there for them to write down what they were most thankful for. Then they would place them anonymously into the small bowl on the table. The supper went amazingly smooth with pleasant conversations, no kitchen emergencies, and a warm vibe among the guests that felt so authentic, as if they had known each other for years.

Once the plates were cleared, I took one piece of paper out of the bowl and read it out loud. I then passed the bowl to one of the guests and each in turn read one of the papers. For me, I was thankful that I had met so many wonderful Brooklynites and brought so many more together.

The Theme

Another autumn had returned to Brooklyn, and I really wanted to celebrate the season, but with a menu that represented my southern roots. The menu was to be truly southern in its ingredients and dishes. I was bringing my roots to the table. Biscuits, trout, pork, apples, and mustard greens would be the humble stars of the dishes. I took a few blankets, a picnic basket, and my Sula-girl to the Brooklyn Bridge park to plan the menu.

The Setup

The long harvest table in my four-story walk-up was dressed in woolen scarves I brought back from India. I scattered acorns, hazelnuts, small decorative pumpkins, and paper leaves across the table. Orange and red Moroccan tea glasses held votive candles. It was exotic yet warming. I served the courses family style for the first time. Cream-colored square dining plates at each chair were topped with a blank piece of paper. In the center of the table was a small cup holding tiny gold pencils.

September's Serenade
(Celebrating the Season in Song
and Savory Seasonal Flavors)

Saturday, September 29th
7:30PM

Cornbread, Olive,
Sun Kissed Tomato Biscuit

September Succotash

Pan Seared Trout;
Peppered Cous Cous,
Roasted Fennel, Lemon Jus

Rosemary Pork Tenderloin;
Wilted Greens, Balsamic Beets,
Mustard Stout Beer Sauce

Apple Pear Cinnamon Cake;
Salted Caramel Apple

5 Courses, $50, Suggested Donation
RSVP via Paypal
First Come, First Seat
BYOB, Wine Pairing on Website
www.hautenthekitchen.com
Location Details Follow Reservation
See you there, *Heather*

Olive, Sun-kissed Tomato Cornbread Biscuits

- 1½ cups plus 2 Tbsp all-purpose flour
- ¼ cup plus 2 Tbsp yellow cornmeal
- 2 tsp baking powder
- ¾ tsp baking soda
- ¾ tsp salt
- 1½ Tbsp sugar
- 6 Tbsp unsalted butter, chilled and cut into ½-inch pieces
- ¾ cup plus 1 Tbsp nonfat buttermilk, divided
- 1 cup kalamata olives, finely chopped
- 1 cup sun dried tomatoes, rinsed if packed in oil and finely chopped

Preheat oven to 400°F.

In a mixing bowl, add flour, cornmeal, baking powder, baking soda, salt, and sugar. Whisk together.

Stir in butter, buttermilk, olives, and tomatoes until well combined with dry ingredients.

On a floured cutting board or surface area, roll out dough until 1 inch thick.

Use an approximately 1-inch round cookie cutter or glass to cut out bite-size biscuit rounds.

Line a baking sheet with parchment paper.

Place biscuit rounds onto paper.

Brush each with extra buttermilk.

Bake 12–15 minutes until golden brown and airy.

Serve as a passed hors d'oeuvre or amuse-bouche.

Pan-Seared Trout with Lemon Jus, Peppered Couscous, Roasted Fennel

Trout

- 1 Tbsp olive oil
- 1 Tbsp butter, unsalted
- 2 whole garlic cloves
- 1 tsp salt
- 1 tsp pepper
- 1 lb trout fillets, rinsed and patted dry
- Juice of 2 lemons

Add oil and butter to a sauté pan.

Add whole garlic cloves and salt and pepper.

Warm to medium heat, stir to combine oil and butter well.

Begin cooking trout fillets turning once in a 6–7-minute period.

Squeeze lemon juice over filets halfway through cooking

Remove cooked filets and place on a paper towel–covered plate.

Cook all fillets, being sure not to overlap them on the plate when removed.

Couscous

- 2 cups couscous
- 1 tsp fresh thyme, finely chopped
- 1 tsp fresh rosemary, finely chopped
- 1 tsp fresh ground black pepper
- ½ tsp each salt and pepper
- 1 cup vegetable stock

Pour couscous into a mixing bowl.

Add fresh herbs, salt, and pepper to the bowl.

In a sauce pan, add vegetable stock and bring to a low boil.

Pour stock gently over couscous until it is just covered.

Let sit while couscous absorbs stock, approximately 5 minutes.

Once absorbed, use a fork to very lightly rake couscous to separate the kernels.

Couscous should become light and fluffy, not soggy or heavy.

Use an ice cream scoop to plate couscous.

Roasted Fennel

- 2 fennel bulbs, fronds removed
- ½ cup olive oil
- Salt and pepper to taste

Place whole fennel bulbs in a baking dish.

Coat with olive oil on all sides and sprinkle with salt and pepper.

Bring oven to 375°F.

Roast fennel for 25–30 minutes until soft and tender.

Remove from oven and cover to keep warm before serving.

When plating, slice each fennel in half lengthwise and place onto serving dish or plates.

Rosemary Pork Tenderloin
Wilted Greens, Balsamic Beets,
Mustard Stout Beer Sauce

Tenderloin

- ½ cup fresh rosemary, finely chopped
- ½ cup plus 2 Tbsp olive oil, divided
- 3 garlic cloves, finely chopped
- 1 tsp salt
- 1 tsp black pepper
- 1½ lb whole pork tenderloin, rinsed and patted dry

Preheat oven to 350°F.

In a small bowl, combine chopped rosemary, ½ cup olive oil, garlic, salt, and pepper.

Coat tenderloin in herb mixture.

Place tenderloin on a cookie tray or baking dish in the oven.

Roast for 40 minutes or until temperature reads 145°F.

Remove and let rest at least 15 minutes before slicing into ½-inch medallions.

Beets

- 4 medium red beets, peeled and cut into quarters
- 1 Tbsp olive oil
- ½ cup balsamic vinegar
- 1 tsp garlic, finely chopped
- Salt and pepper to taste

Toss quartered beets with olive oil, vinegar, garlic, salt, and pepper.

Roast on same or separate baking dish in oven with the pork.

Greens

- 1 Tbsp olive oil
- 1 tsp red chili flakes
- 2 lb dark leafy greens mix (kale, spinach, chard)
- ½ cup white wine
- Salt and pepper to taste

In a saucepan, add olive oil and chili flakes.

Bring to medium heat and add leafy greens. Greens can be roughly chopped or kept whole, but remove stems if there are any.

Pour white wine over greens, cover with lid and let wilt until soft and tender, approximately 10 minutes.

Taste for salt and pepper.

Sauce

- ½ cup Dijon mustard
- 2 cups stout beer
- ½ cup beef stock
- ½ tsp flour
- ½ cup water
- Salt and pepper to taste

In a saucepan, combine Dijon, beer, and stock.

Mix well and bring to medium heat.

In a cup, combine flour and water. Stir until completely combined with no lumps.

Add flour mixture to sauce and stir constantly making sure it does not lump.

Sauce consistency should be creamy and thick with no visible flour.

Season with salt and pepper to taste.

On serving plates or a platter, fan the pork tenderloin medallions on top of each other, three to an individual dinner plate. Fork wilted greens on the side along with a spoonful of beets. Drizzle mustard sauce over pork medallions.

Serve.

Apple Pear Cinnamon Cake,
Salted Caramel Sauce

Apple Cinnamon Cake

- 2 Granny Smith apples, peeled and thinly sliced

- 2 tsp lemon juice

- 1 cup plus 4 Tbsp sugar, divided

- 1½ tsp cinnamon

- ¾ cup butter, unsalted and softened

- 1 tsp vanilla

- 3 eggs

- 3½ Tbsp vegetable oil

- ¾ cup plus 2 Tbsp milk

- 2½ cups flour

- 1 tsp cinnamon

- 2 tsp baking powder

Preheat oven to 350°F.

Lightly grease and flour a 9-inch cake pan with olive oil.

In a mixing bowl, combine apple slices and lemon juice.

Set aside.

In a separate small mixing bowl, combine cinnamon and 4 tablespoons sugar.

In a third mixing bowl, combine butter and 1 cup sugar. Cream them together.

Add eggs, 1 at a time to the butter mixture.

Combine, then add oil, vanilla, and milk.

Combine all until smooth.

Pour batter into cake pan.

Top with apple slices in a slightly overlapping circular pattern.

Sprinkle cinnamon sugar over apples.

Bake for one hour, until a toothpick comes out clean.

Serve warm with salted caramel sauce.

Salted Caramel Sauce

- 1 cup sugar

- ¼ cup cold water

- ½ cup heavy cream

- 2 Tbsp butter, unsalted

- ¾ tsp salt

Over the course of hosting my suppers, at some point I added a little takeaway for my guests. I had made this caramel sauce and one guest commented that it was so good you wanted more than just the drizzle over the dessert. He called it "crack caramel," and so it was coined. From then on, for each place setting, I put a small, cloth, drawstring bag on each napkin. Inside was a small pretzel covered in the caramel sauce and cooled until it hardened. It was the perfect last bite on the way home.

In a saucepan combine sugar and ¼ cup cold water.

Set over medium heat, stir to combine.

Heat for 10 minutes, without stirring.

Sugar should turn amber in color.

Meanwhile warm cream in a saucepan.

When caramelized sugar is ready, slowly whisk in cream until smooth.

Remove from heat and add butter and salt.

Whisk until creamy and smooth.

About the Author

Heather Antonelli knew from an early age that she wanted to see the world. Through her career as the owner of a product development and sourcing firm in the international home furnishings industry, she has been able to achieve that.

While her passion is travel, her first stops in any new destination are the food markets. There, she can discover new flavors, new ingredients, and new dishes to create for friends and family. India, China, Vietnam, Indonesia, and South Africa are just a few places where she draws inspiration for new recipes.

While living in Brooklyn, New York, Heather started a supper club to continue sharing her cooking with others. For each supper, she created the theme and menu, publicized it on her website and blog, and welcomed over a dozen guests to her long, decorated dining table in her brownstone apartment. The dinners were a hit, with tickets often selling out in forty-eight hours.

Antonelli is the author of another cookbook, *Haute in the Kitchen*. At home, she enjoys cooking for friends and family, sharing her new discoveries. She now lives in southern California and enjoys cooking with her four-year-old daughter.